Contemporary COOKING

Volume 2

Contemporary COOKING

Volume 2

3M

Contemporary Cooking

Editorial production by James Charlton Associates, Ltd. New York. Editor-in-Chief, James Charlton; Managing Editors, Barbara Binswanger, Jennie McGregor; Food Editors, Inez M. Krech, Cecile Lamalle, Anne Lanigan, Maria Robbins.

Book production and manufacturing consulting by:
Cobb/Dunlop Publishing Services, Inc., New York
Art Direction and interior design by:
Marsha Cohen/Parallelogram

Acknowledgments: Pat Cocklin, Delu PAL International, Alan Duns, John Elliott, Melvin Grey, Gina Harris, Anthony Kay, Paul Kemp, David Levin, David Meldrum, Roger Phillips, Nick Powell, Iain Reid, John Turner, Paul Williams, Herbert Wise, George Wright, Cuisinarts, Inc.

Printed and bound in Yugoslavia.

Library of Congress Cataloging in Publication Data
Main entry under title:

Contemporary Cooking.

Includes index.
1. Cookery. I. Minnesota Mining and Manufacturing Company.
TX715.C7586 1984 641.5 84-2563
0-88159-500-4 — (set)
ISBN: 0-88159–001–0

CONTENTS

for the Contemporary Cooking Series

VOLUME 2

Part One

OMELETS AND QUICHES

The egg is probably the closest thing there is to an all-purpose ingredient. The Encyclopaedia Britannica says that, "Considering all factors, eggs rank next after milk in importance and efficiency among foods of animal origin."

It is the traditional emergency food of those who can't cook, and one of the most treasured resources of those who love to cook. Depending on how it is used, it will lighten, thicken, emulsify, coat, bind, gild, raise, and impart various nuances of flavor and texture. Eggs are the basis of one whole family of sauces and a fine enrichment of many others; they can thicken cream soups or be floated in delicate threads in broths. So nutritionally superior are eggs in themselves that a small amount can transform starchy staples such as pasta and rice into protein-rich meals. In one form or another they can be eaten as the mainstay of any meal of the day, and all of their three major components—yolk, white, and shell—have important uses extending far beyond the kitchen.

The usefulness of the egg is a direct reflection of what it biologically *is*: the complete reservoir of nutrition that an embryo chick will draw on from laying to hatching, packaged in concentrated form within a well-constructed shield. Eggs were among the first foods from which early chemists began to deduce the existence of what are now called proteins, and the very name for protein in some languages is identical with that for egg white. To this day, they remain the standard by which nutritionists measure the biological value of other protein sources.

The best eggs are the freshest, whether they are white, brown, or speckled. The color of the shell is determined by the breed of the hen and has nothing to do with the goodness or "naturalness" of what is inside. However, there are other ways of judging quality. Really fresh eggs feel

OMELETS

The perfect French omelet is just cooked on the outside and creamily runny on the inside (the French call this *baveuse*), with just the touch of flavor from the filling. Such an omelet makes a perfect light meal. Serve it straight from the pan, with a delicious salad, French bread and sweet butter. Or have crusty brown bread and thin slices of ham. Omelets provide the ideal way to make a quick meal, or to stretch a meal when unexpected guests arrive, or to use small amounts of leftovers—cheese, fish or meat, mushrooms, tomatoes. For sweet omelets, good for breakfast or light desserts, use jam, marmalade or fruit purée for filling.

Special Pointers

The eggs for omelets must be as fresh as possible, to give good volume. Large eggs are the best size.

For better texture and volume, let eggs reach room temperature before you start; allow an hour for this.

If you are serving more than 2 people, plan on making omelets in batches. An omelet made with more than 4 eggs requires too large a pan for comfortable handling, and the bulk of the ingredients makes it hard to have an omelet of good texture.

Omelets are made in a matter of seconds and they wait for no one. Guests should be ready and warmed plates should be at hand for the omelets.

Making the Omelet

The equipment needed for making an omelet is minimal and is strictly a matter of personal taste.

The classic omelet pan is supposedly never used for anything else and is never washed but only cleaned with paper and salt. Such a pan, made of black cast iron, with numbers stamped on the handle, is unfortunately heavy for an average woman's hand, which is the chief disadvantage. But any pan with sloping sides and a heavy smooth flat base can be used; and indeed you may wash it all you like.

Break eggs into a bowl and let them reach room temperature. Stir with a fork just enough to break yolks and mix yolks and whites together. Stir water into eggs. Add half of the herbs if you are using them. Place butter in the omelet pan set over high heat. When butter melts, swirl it around to coat sides and bottom. Butter will foam up, then foam will subside. At that point, pour in the eggs; do not wait until butter starts to brown. Let eggs cook for 1 second, then stir with the flat of the fork or a spatula. After 1 second, reduce heat to just below medium. Lift edge of omelet and let the still liquid part run underneath. Slide the pan back and forth; you should feel the omelet sliding around, a sure sign that it is almost cooked. At this point, sprinkle filling over half of the omelet; the eggs should still be creamy and slightly runny. Tilt the pan away from you so that part of the omelet slides up the side of the pan. Use a spatula to flip this part over the filling. Lift pan from heat, and turn it over, depositing omelet on a warmed plate. Or place the plate over the pan and invert both together. Omelets should be eaten at once; if they have to be kept hot, they will be overcooked.

Fillings for Omelets

A basic omelet lends itself to countless varieties of fillings, both savory and sweet. Here are just a few:

Au Fromage. Sprinkle 3 tablespoons grated Gruyère or Cheddar cheese over omelet when it begins to set. Fold in half and serve.

Bonne Femme. Sauté 2 tablespoons minced onion, 1 lean bacon

French Omelet

2 portions

3 large eggs
1 tablespoon cold water
1 tablespoon unsalted butter
2 tablespoons chopped fresh parsley, chives and thyme, (optional)

• Eggs will absorb odors through their shells. So take a tip from the French and store your eggs in a bag along with the fresh herbs you will use in your omelet.

Set pan over high heat. Swirl butter around to coat bottom and sides.

When all liquid egg has run underneath, let pan rest flat again over the heat.

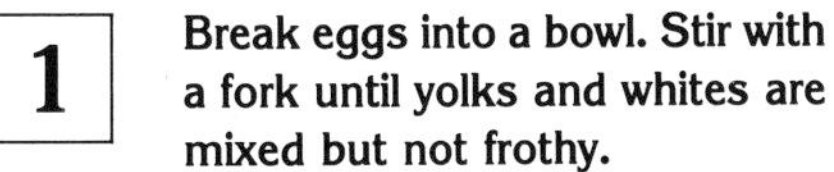

1 Break eggs into a bowl. Stir with a fork until yolks and whites are mixed but not frothy.

2 Add 1 tablespoon cold water and stir with the fork to mix. Add half of herb mixture if you use herbs.

3 Place butter in an omelet pan no larger than 10 inches across, with sloping sides and heavy bottom.

5 When foaming subsides and butter is about to color, pour in the eggs. Leave for 1 second.

6 Stir eggs with the flat side of a fork about 3 times. Leave for 1 second. Reduce heat.

7 Using a spatula, lift the edge of the omelet and tilt the pan to let liquid eggs run underneath the cooked portion.

9 Sprinkle prepared filling over half of the surface of the omelet.

10 Tilt the pan away from you and with the spatula flip the uncovered half of the omelet over the filling. Season, if desired.

11 Place a warmed serving plate over the pan and invert both together. Sprinkle omelet with remaining herbs if you use them.

slice, diced, and 3 sliced fresh mushrooms in 1 tablespoon butter for 3 minutes.

Chasseur. Sauté 2 tablespoons minced shallots in 1 tablespoon butter for 2 minutes. Add 4 mushrooms, sliced thin; sauté for 1 minute. Add 2 tablespoons dry white wine; bring to a boil. Cook for 1 minute.

Jubilee Omelet. Fill with 2 tablespoons black cherry jam mixed with 2 teaspoons Kirsch liqueur.

Niçoise. Sauté 2 tablespoons chopped onion and 1 garlic clove, crushed, in 1 tablespoon olive oil for 4 minutes. Add 1 chopped large tomato, 2 chopped anchovy fillets and 6 chopped pitted black olives. Sauté for 3 minutes.

Pain Perdu. Fill with croutons, fried until crisp, and minced fresh parsley.

Strawberry Omelet. Heat 2 tablespoons strawberry jam in a small heavy pan. Add with a few halved strawberries.

Sweet omelets are often dusted with a little superfine or granulated sugar before serving. They can be put under the broiler for a few seconds to caramelize the sugar.

Soufflé Omelets and Flat Omelets

Soufflé omelets are light and fluffy, a cross between a standard French omelet and a soufflé. They are most often served as desserts. Flat omelets include the Italian *frittata,* Spanish *tortilla,* Arab *eggah.* These are all filling and hearty and much simpler to make than the others since they are cooked until set and not folded or rolled. While classic omelets are cooked over brisk heat, both soufflé and flat omelets are cooked over moderate heat and finished under a broiler or in the oven.

The prepared filling for flat omelets is mixed with the eggs and both are cooked together.

Flat Omelets

These omelets are cut into wedges to serve; usually an 8-inch *frittata* or *tortilla* will make 4 portions. A *frittata* is usually savory, but there are recipes for sweet ones too.

Allow 2 eggs per serving and have them at room temperature. Do not plan to cook more than 6 eggs in a pan at a time.

Liquid is not used in these flat omelets.

Cook savory *frittata* and *tortilla* in olive or corn oil. Use 2 tablespoons oil for 4 eggs.

Sweet flat omelets use butter only, preferably clarified butter. Use 4 tablespoons for 4 eggs.

Fillings for sweet and savory omelets are cooked in the omelet pan, or reheated in it if they are cooked already.

Chinese Omelets

Chinese omelets fall halfway between delicate French omelets and the more robust *tortillas* of Spain and *eggahs* of Arab countries. Chinese omelets can be kept warm over simmering water for some time, so it is possible to make them to serve more than 2 people at a time. These omelets, or *foo yung,* can be served as a first course or main course, plain or with a sauce, or they can be cut into strips or shreds to decorate or mix into fried rice.

In these omelets eggs serve as a binder for the filling, therefore 6 large eggs can make a Chinese omelet for 4 portions. No liquid is mixed with the eggs, but sherry or soy sauce is mixed with the filling; these two flavorings are Chinese favorites. An egg *foo yung* is fried in oil rather than butter, and the first choice is sesame seed oil. Lacking that, use another seed oil or as a last resort corn oil. Allow 1 teaspoon oil for each egg in the omelet.

Egg Foo Yung (Chinese

4 portions

- **6 eggs**
- **1 cup diced cooked chicken, meat or fish**
- **2 scallions**
- **2 slices of gingerroot**
- **¾ cup bean sprouts**
- **3 tablespoons sesame seed oil or corn oil**
- **1 tablespoon dry sherry**
- **1 tablespoon soy sauce**

4 **Stir-fry the filling in the oil for 1 minute. Pour in sherry and soy sauce. Remove from heat.**

7 **Leave pan over brisk heat for 1 minute, until the bottom of the omelet is set.**

Omelet)

1 Break the eggs into a bowl and beat with a whisk or rotary beater until frothy.

2 Prepare filling. Shred meat. Sliver scallions. Peel and mince gingerroot. Add bean sprouts.

3 Heat 2 teaspoons of the oil in a skillet or wok over brisk heat.

5 Mix filling with beaten eggs. Heat remaining oil in a 10- to 12-inch skillet, or part of the oil in a 5-inch skillet.

6 Pour one quarter of the omelet batter into the small pan and stir once.

OR Pour all the omelet batter into the large pan and stir once.

8 Place a lightly oiled plate over the skillet and invert pan and plate together.

9 Slide omelet back into the skillet, uncooked side down, and cook for another minute, or until done to your taste.

10 Invert cooked omelet on a plate. Set it over a pan of barely simmering water if there is delay in serving. Cover.

Fillings

The fillings for these omelets are stir-fried briefly; they should remain crisp-crunchy rather than tender as they will be cooked further as the omelet is cooked. Fillings can be slivers of cooked ham, chicken, pork or beef; flaked fish or shellfish; vegetables such as bean sprouts, scallions, mushrooms, zucchini, red or green peppers; the vegetables should be chopped or shredded. When the filling has been stir-fried, sherry and/or soy sauce are added. Use 1 tablespoon dry sherry or soy sauce to the filling for a 6-egg omelet. Minced fresh gingerroot and garlic are sometimes used to give greater pungency to the filling.

To make a large omelet, use a 10- to 12-inch skillet with sloping sides. For individual omelets, use a 5-inch pan.

Break eggs into a bowl and beat with a whisk or rotary beater until frothy. (This is different from the French style, in which the eggs are beaten only to mix them.)

Prepare filling ingredients, slicing, chopping or shredding them. Small vegetables and shellfish (shrimps) are left whole. Meat should be cut into slivers. Crab meat or fish should be flaked. Gingerroot and garlic should be peeled and minced.

Heat 2 to 3 teaspoons oil in a small skillet or wok and stir-fry the filling ingredients for 1 minute. Add sherry and/or soy sauce.

Mix the filling into the beaten eggs.

Heat remaining oil in a large skillet for a large omelet, or pour a small amount of oil into a small skillet for an individual omelet.

Ladle a quarter of the omelet batter into the small pan, or all of it into the large pan.

Let the omelet cook for 1 minute, until the bottom is set. Do not stir or lift the omelet.

Place an oiled plate over the pan and turn pan and plate over together. Slide omelet back into the pan, uncooked side down.

Cook for 1 minute longer, or until omelet is cooked to your taste. Invert the finished omelet on a warm plate, divide into portions, garnish with watercress sprigs or fringed scallions.

Soufflé Omelets

For these the eggs are separated and whites beaten until almost stiff, thus making a very bulky omelet.

Use 3 medium-size eggs for 2 portions and have them at room temperature.

Use only 1 tablespoon liquid for 3 eggs; if liqueur is used, do not add water as it would make the omelet too runny.

Always cook these in unsalted butter. Use ½ tablespoon butter for each egg.

For sweet omelets, add 1 tablespoon sugar for 3 eggs.

Raw ingredients must be cooked. If you are macerating fruit, do this at least 3 hours before you plan to make the omelet.

When separating eggs, use 2 clean dry bowls. Do not let even the tiniest particle of egg yolk escape into the bowl of whites, for then it would not be possible to beat the whites stiff.

Add a pinch of salt to egg whites and beat them with a whisk, rotary beater or electric mixer until they form soft peaks when the beater is withdrawn. Do not beat until whites are dry.

Pour the yolk mixture on the egg whites and fold in with a metal spoon or spatula so they are evenly distributed.

Use firm light movements; do not stir, for stirring breaks up the air bubbles you have just beaten into the whites.

• *Serving suggestions:* a sweet soufflé omelet makes a fine dessert that is ready in minutes. Serve it to balance a light soup and salad dinner or lunch.

• Substitute orange rind for the lemon. Heat a few drops of Grand Marnier and pour over the finished omelet.

• Split a vanilla bean and store it in your sugar canister for delicious vanilla-flavored sugar toppings.

Sweet Soufflé Omelet

2 portions

- **1 lemon**
- **3 large eggs**
- **1 tablespoon granulated sugar**
- **pinch of salt**
- **1½ tablespoons unsalted butter**
- **superfine sugar for top of omelet**

2 Separate eggs into 2 bowls, making sure no yolk falls into the bowl of whites

6 Heat butter in an 8-inch omelet pan set over moderate heat. Swirl the butter around the pan to coat sides and bottom.

1 Preheat broiler to its highest temperature. Grate lemon rind and squeeze the juice.

3 Add grated lemon rind, 1 tablespoon juice and the granulated sugar to the egg yolks. Mix well.

4 Add a pinch of salt to egg whites and beat them until they stand in soft peaks when beater is withdrawn.

5 Pour yolk mixture into whites and fold with a metal spoon until evenly distributed.

7 When butter stops foaming, pour in egg mixture. Cook until it is set on the bottom.

8 Place pan under the preheated broiler and cook for 30 seconds to set the top of the omelet.

9 Flip half of the omelet over the other half with a spatula. Turn out onto a warmed plate.

Filling and Garnishing a Soufflé Omelet

1 *Solid Filling:* Make a depression across the center of the omelet with a spatula.

2 Place filling in the depression. Flip one side of omelet over the other, using the spatula to turn it, and serve at once.

1 *Jam Filling:* When omelet has been finished under the broiler, spread jam filling over half of the surface with a flexible spatula.

OR *Fresh Fruit Filling:* Reserve some of the fruit and arrange it around the curved edge of the folded soufflé omelet.

OR *Glazed Omelet:* Sprinkle top with superfine sugar, then slide under the heated broiler for 30 seconds to caramelize sugar.

OR *Patterned Glazing:* Sprinkle finished omelet with superfine sugar. Caramelize with a heated skewer to make crisscross lines.

QUICHES

A quiche is an open tart in a pastry crust with a savory custard filling. The shell is made of short-crust pastry (French *pâte brisée*).

Quiche makes a delicious first course, at its best just hot from the oven. Small squares or wedges of cold quiche can be served as cocktail food, or for buffet meals. For a lunch or supper, a hot quiche and a salad make a complete meal.

Baking Tart Pastry

Quiches may be baked in any tart or pie pan you have, but it is easiest to serve them from a French tart pan with a removable bottom. These pans have fluted sides, which give the finished tart a decorative appearance. Another good choice is a porcelain quiche dish; they come in various sizes and are the perfect choice when you plan to serve the quiche in its dish, hot from the oven.

The pastry shell for a custard tart is partially baked before it is filled, to prevent the moist custard sinking into the pastry and making it soggy. This step is called "baking blind." Shortcrust pastry is so buttery, it is not essential to grease the pan or dish, but it is never a mistake to rub it with a very light coating of oil or butter.

Make the pastry and roll it out to a round 1½ inches wider all around than the diameter of the pan or dish.

Roll the dough on the rolling pin, then unroll it over the pan and carefully center it, without stretching it.

Work from the center out to fit pastry snugly into the bottom and the fluted sides; be sure there are no pockets of air trapped between pastry and pan.

Let any excess pastry hang over the rim, then roll the pin straight over it, to cut off these bits. Rolling is better than cutting. As the edge will be a little ragged, pinch any ragged edge between thumb and forefinger and again press it firmly against the pan.

Cover the pastry-filled pan loosely and slide into the refrigerator for 30 minutes to 1 hour.

Preheat oven to 400°F.

Prick the pastry with a fork all over to release any air bubbles.

Cut a circle of foil or wax paper about 3 inches larger than the diameter of the pan, and gently press it into the pastry-lined pan, fitting it into the fluted sides. Fill it with dried beans or rice; or use ceramic or aluminum pie weights. Be sure weights are pushed firmly against the sides.

Bake the weighted pastry for 10 minutes.

Remove from oven and carefully lift out foil or paper with its load of pellets.

Return pan to the oven and bake for 3 to 5 minutes longer, until pastry is set but not noticeably colored.

To bake the crust completely, return it to the oven for approximately 5 to 10 minutes after removing the lining.

Filling Quiches

The custard for quiche traditionally includes cream. Use light or heavy cream, according to the richness of the filling you plan. For a thinner custard, use half-and-half. For an 8-inch quiche, you will need 2 medium-size eggs and 1 cup light cream; for a richer custard, use egg yolks only, or add an extra yolk to the whole eggs.

The flavoring ingredient can be mixed into the custard, but it is more usual to layer it in the pastry, then gently pour in the custard. It should come just below the top of the pastry sides to allow room for the filling to puff up.

If any of the flavoring ingredients needs long cooking, cook it partially or completely before adding, since too long cooking of the custard makes it dry on top.

At the end of cooking time the filling should be risen and well browned. To test that the filling is cooked, insert a fine skewer into its center—it should come out clean.

If you want your quiche to have an appetizing, shiny, dark brown surface, sprinkle a little grated cheese over the top of the filling.

Cheese. Hard cheeses can be grated or sliced; soft cheeses can be mashed or crumbled, or spread on the pastry. Cheese can be mixed with vegetables for delicious variations. Cheddar, Emmental, Gruyère, Parmesan, Romano, Edam, Gouda, Monterey Jack are good. Also cottage and farmer cheese, cream cheese, goat cheese, plain or mixed with herbs. Blue cheeses (Stilton, Roquefort, Gorgonzola, Danish Blue) are pungent; add some of any of these to milder cheeses.

Fish. Since fish cooks quickly, there is no need to precook it. Remove skin and bones and cut fish into small pieces. Smoked fish is also good with custard. Canned fish and shellfish—tuna, salmon, crab, shrimps—are convenient for fillings. Drain them well and flake if necessary. If shrimps are very salty, rinse them.

Meat. The classic meat for quiche Lorraine is thick smoky bacon. Ham and sausages are also good. Chicken or turkey can be used. Any raw meat should be cooked. Bacon should be about half cooked to eliminate a large part of the fat.

Vegetables. Should be chopped or cut into thin slices. Except for tomatoes, bell peppers, scallions and other mild onions, vegetables should be cooked until crunchy-tender; either steam them or sweat in butter; drain them well to prevent diluting the custard.

Serving Quiche

Try to serve the quiche within 10 minutes or the puff will sink. If you have a pan with removable bottom, set it on an upturned bowl and gently push off the ring. Slide the quiche from the metal bottom onto a warmed serving dish.

If you plan to serve the quiche cold, remove the ring in the same way, while quiche is still hot, and slide it from the bottom onto a wire rack to let steam evaporate, which would soften the pastry.

A cold quiche or, more accurately, a quiche at room temperature, can be delicious and makes perfect picnic fare.

You can certainly reheat a quiche, although it will never puff up again.

Filled quiches freeze well for 2 months and are a particularly useful standby as they are one of the few dishes that can be served within a short time of being taken out of the freezer.

To heat, unwrap the frozen quiche and stand it on a baking sheet. Place the frozen quiche in the oven, heated to 425°F and cook for 20 minutes. Then cover the top loosely with foil to prevent overbrowning and cook for another 20 minutes at 350°F or until hot right through to the center.

If you prefer, you can thaw the quiche. This will take 6 to 8 hours at room temperature, or overnight in the refrigerator.

Classic Quiche Lorraine

4 portions

5 ounces Short-Crust Pastry (see Index)
4 ounces thick smoky bacon
2 eggs
⅔ cup light cream
salt
freshly ground pepper
pinch of grated nutmeg

• Don't hesitate to sprinkle a few tablespoons of freshly grated Parmesan cheese on top before baking.
• Served with a tossed green salad and a chilled white wine, a Quiche Lorraine makes an elegant lunch.

1 Put oven shelf above the center and preheat oven to 400°F. Line 8-inch flan pan with pastry, bake blind until partially done.

2 Remove any rind from bacon; chop strips into small pieces. Cook over moderate heat until fat has been rendered.

3 Use a slotted spoon to lift bacon from pan to kitchen paper towels to drain; arrange the pieces in the pastry-lined pan.

4 Make custard: Beat eggs lightly, stir in cream; season. (Remember bacon has own saltiness.) Beat until well blended.

5 Strain custard, then pour it carefully into the pan without disturbing the bacon. Filling should come just below the edge.

6 Bake for about 25 minutes, or until filling is cooked. Test by inserting a skewer in the center; it should come out clean.

7 Stand pan on an upside-down bowl and let the ring slide off. If serving hot, slide quiche off base onto warmed serving plate.

8 If serving cold, slide quiche onto a rack to cool. Slide a spatula between base of pan and pastry to loosen it.

Petits Domaines

Country Omelet with Ham and Potato

2 portions

- **2 ounces fresh sorrel**
- **1 ounce unsalted butter**
- **4 large eggs**
- **pepper**
- **4 ounces ham or prosciutto**
- **1 small new potato, cooked**

Cut coarse stem ends from the sorrel and discard any yellowing leaves. Wash well in several waters and shake dry. Place sorrel in a heavy pan over medium heat with half of the butter. Cover the pan and cook sorrel for 5 minutes, turning from time to time so all leaves are cooked. Meanwhile, break the eggs into a large bowl and stir with a fork until well mixed but not frothy. Season with pepper to taste. (Use no salt as the ham is salty.) Add 1 tablespoon cold water and mix again. Cut the ham into small strips and add to the sorrel. Cut cooked potato into small cubes and add also. Cover the pan and keep the filling warm.

Put remaining butter in a 10-inch omelet pan over high heat. Turn the pan so that the butter swirls around and coats all sides. When the foam has subsided, pour in the eggs. Leave for 1 second, then stir with the flat of a fork or with a spatula. Leave for another second, then reduce heat to medium. Lift the edge of the omelet to let the uncooked portion run underneath. When the omelet is cooked to your taste, put the filling on half of it and flip the uncovered half over the filling. Tilt the pan to let the omelet slide out. Divide it and serve at once.

Little Summer Omelets

8 portions

- **2 tablespoons cream cheese**
- **6 watercress sprigs**
- **3 small firm tomatoes**
- **1 small onion**
- **4 parsley sprigs**
- **salt and pepper**
- **2 ounces fresh lima beans or other shell beans**
- **2 tablespoons heavy cream**
- **8 large eggs**
- **1½ ounces unsalted butter**

Make the fillings: Cream cheese and watercress: In a small bowl beat the cream cheese with a wooden spoon until soft. Trim coarse stems from watercress and any yellowing leaves. Wash leaves and roll in a towel to dry. Chop leaves fine and stir into the cream cheese.

Tomato and onion: Peel tomatoes, chop, and place in a bowl. Peel and chop the onion and add to tomatoes. Chop parsley and add. Season with salt and pepper to taste and mix well.

Shell beans and cream: Place lima beans or other fresh shell beans in a saucepan of water and simmer until just tender. Drain well and transfer to a bowl. Mix in the cream.

Break the eggs into a large bowl and stir with a fork until well mixed but not frothy. Add 2 tablespoons cold water and mix again. Season to taste. Place 1 teaspoon of the butter in a 5-inch omelet pan over high heat. As the butter melts, turn the pan so that butter swirls around and coats all sides. When the foam has subsided, pour in 3 tablespoons of the egg mixture. Stir eggs with the flat of a kitchen fork about 3 times. Leave for 1 second, then reduce heat to medium. Using a spatula, lift the edge of the omelet to let uncooked egg run underneath. When the omelet is just cooked, place 2 tablespoons of any filling on half of it and turn the other half over to cover the filling. With a pancake turner, lift out the omelet to a cold serving plate; or invert the omelet pan to turn out the finished omelet.

Continue in this way until all the omelet batter and all the fillings have been used. Leave omelets in a cool place until ready to be served, but do not keep for more than 6 hours or the fillings will become watery. Serve 1 omelet as a snack or first course. If you plan to serve them as part of a main course, make more, to allow 2 omelets per person.

French Cheese Omelet

2 portions

- **4 large eggs**
- **salt and pepper**
- **1 tablespoon grated Parmesan cheese**
- **1 ounce Gruyère cheese**
- **2 tablespoons heavy cream**
- **1 tablespoon unsalted butter**

Break the eggs into a large bowl and stir with a fork until well mixed but not frothy. Season to taste. Add 1 tablespoon cold water and mix again. Stir in the grated Parmesan cheese. Cut Gruyère cheese into tiny cubes and mix with the cream.

Melt the butter in a 10-inch omelet pan over high heat. As it melts turn the pan so butter swirls around and coats all sides. When the foam subsides, pour in the eggs. Leave for 1 second, then stir 3 times with the flat of the fork. Leave for another second, then reduce the heat to medium. Lift the edge of the omelet to let the uncooked egg run underneath. When the omelet is cooked to your taste, place the Gruyère filling over half of it and with a spatula turn the other half over the filling. Place a warmed serving plate over the pan and turn plate and pan over together. Divide the omelet and serve at once.

Italian Cheese Omelet

4 portions

- **6 large eggs**
- **salt and pepper**
- **1 cup ricotta cheese**
- **3 tablespoons grated Parmesan cheese**
- **⅛ teaspoon crumbled dried orégano**
- **1 ounce unsalted butter**

Break the eggs into a large bowl, add 1 tablespoon cold water and salt and pepper to taste, and beat well with a fork until completely mixed but not frothy. Combine the two cheeses and stir in the orégano.

Melt the butter in a 10-inch omelet pan over high heat. When it stops foaming, pour in the eggs and cook for 1 minute. Then reduce heat to medium and lift the edge of the eggs to let the uncooked portion run underneath. With a metal spatula loosen the omelet around the edges. When it is done to your taste, spoon the cheese mixture on half of it, then with the spatula flip the other half over the filling. Serve at once. Tomato sauce is good with this omelet.

Crab and Ginger Foo Yung

4 portions

- **6 large eggs**
- **4 ounces crab meat**
- **1½ ounces fresh gingerroot**
- **2 green onions (scallions)**
- **3 tablespoons sesame seed oil**
- **1 tablespoon soy sauce**
- **1 tablespoon dry sherry**

Break the eggs into a large bowl and beat with a fork until frothy. Flake the crab meat, removing any bits of cartilage. Peel the gingerroot and mince it. Trim green onions and chop fine. Heat 2 teaspoons of the oil in a small heavy pan over high heat. Add crab meat, ginger, soy sauce and sherry. Stir-fry for 1 minute, then remove from heat. Mix the crab mixture into the bowl of eggs.

Heat remaining oil in a 10-inch omelet pan. Pour in one quarter of the egg mixture. Stir once to distribute the filling and cook for 1 minute. Invert a dinner plate over the pan and turn pan and plate over so that the omelet falls on the plate. Slide the omelet back into the pan and cook on the other side for a further minute. Turn out the finished omelet on a plate and set the plate over a pan of boiling water. Cover with another plate to keep it warm until ready to serve.

Cook remaining egg mixture in the same way. Use a little more oil if necessary to finish the omelets.

Variations: For spring *foo yung,* fill the omelet with 2 ounces bean sprouts; 1 ounce button mushrooms, sliced thin; 2 green onions, trimmed and chopped; and 1 ounce lettuce, shredded. For chicken and almond *foo yung,* fill with 4 ounces cooked chicken and 1 ounce slivered blanched almonds. For shrimp *foo yung,* fill with 4 ounces cooked shrimps, chopped, and 2 green onions, trimmed and chopped. Serve with sweet-and-sour sauce. For ham *foo yung,* fill with 4 ounces cooked ham, cut into thin slivers; 2 teaspoons snipped fresh chives; and 2 ounces bean sprouts.

Zucchini Frittata

6 portions

- **1 pound tiny zucchini, about 4 ounces each**
- **3 shallots**
- **2 tablespoons olive oil**
- **1 ounce butter**
- **6 large eggs**
- **salt and pepper**
- **2 ounces Parmesan cheese**
- **8 ounces plum tomatoes**
- **2 tablespoons minced fresh parsley**

Wash and trim zucchini, and cut across into ¼-inch rounds. Peel and mince shallots. Heat oil and butter in a 10-inch skillet or omelet pan and sauté shallots until golden. Add zucchini slices and sauté until they are beginning to brown on the edges. Beat the eggs in a large bowl and season with salt and pepper. Leaving the oil and butter in the skillet, lift out the vegetables and mix them with the eggs.

Preheat broiler. Bring the skillet to high heat and pour in the frittata batter. At once reduce heat and let the frittata cook very slowly until set on the bottom. Grate the cheese. Blanch and peel the tomatoes, chop them, and mix with parsley. Transfer the skillet to the broiler and broil until the top of the frittata is set. Remove from the broiler, sprinkle with the cheese, and cut into wedges to serve. Garnish each portion with some of the tomatoes.

The Pharaoh's Eggah

An eggah is an Arab omelet, rather thick and firm, more like a Spanish tortilla than a French omelet, and it is stuffed with filling.

4 portions

- **2 tablespoons olive oil**
- **8 ounces tender boneless beef or lamb, chopped**
- **1 small onion**
- **1 teaspoon ground cardamom**
- **4 large eggs**
- **salt and pepper**

Heat the oil in an 8-inch frying pan over medium heat. Place meat in the pan and cook, breaking it apart with a fork and stirring to be sure all sides are browned. Peel the onion and chop fine. Add to the frying pan; also add the cardamom. Stir and cook for 5 minutes longer.

Break the eggs into a bowl and stir with a fork until well mixed. Season with salt and pepper to taste. Remove the pan of meat from the heat and carefully pour off as much fat as possible. Return the pan to the heat and pour in the eggs. Stir once so the meat is well distributed. Set the broiler to the highest temperature. Cook the *eggah* for about 3 minutes, until the bottom has set and is firm. Remove pan from the heat and place under the broiler. Broil for about 3 minutes, until the top is also set and firm.

Variations: For eggplant *eggah,* cut a large eggplant into cubes, sprinkle them with salt, and let the cubes drain for 30 minutes. Rinse, pat dry, and fry in oil for about 3 minutes before adding the beaten eggs. Garlic is usually added to eggplant *eggah.* For leek *eggah,* thoroughly wash 2 to 4 young thin leeks and slice them. Fry in oil for 10 minutes, turning often, until golden. Add 2 teaspoons minced parsley to the egg mixture before adding it to the leeks. Top with grated cheese before sliding the pan under the broiler. This is delicious served cold. For mushroom *eggah,* sauté 4 ounces whole mushroom caps and their chopped stems in oil. Add a crushed garlic clove and sauté for another minute. Pour in the eggs. Top with thin slices of tomato and some grated cheese before sliding the pan under the broiler.

Hoppelpoppel

4 portions

- **8 slices of lean bacon**
- **4 cooked medium-size potatoes**
- **1 medium-size onion**
- **1 tablespoon vegetable oil**
- **1 ounce unsalted butter**
- **8 large eggs**
- **3 tablespoons light cream**
- **½ teaspoon salt**
- **½ teaspoon black pepper**
- **½ teaspoon crumbled dried dill**

Chop the bacon. Peel potatoes and cut into thin slices. Peel and chop the onion. Heat the oil in a large skillet over medium heat and cook the bacon until browned and beginning to crisp. Use a slotted spoon to transfer bacon to paper towels to drain. Pour off the fat in the skillet and add the butter. Melt butter over medium heat. Add onion and cook, stirring occasionally, for 4 minutes, until translucent. Add potatoes and cook for 5 minutes, until they are lightly browned.

In a large bowl beat the eggs, cream, salt, pepper and dill until well blended. Stir cooked bacon pieces into the eggs, and pour the whole thing over the vegetables in the skillet. Cook the omelet over low heat, shaking the skillet and stirring the eggs with a fork, until eggs have set. Remove pan from heat. Cut hoppelpoppel into 4 portions and serve at once.

Chicken Liver Quiche

4 to 6 portions

5 ounces Short-Crust Pastry (see Index)
4 ounces chicken livers
salt
2 ounces butter
4 tablespoons Madeira wine
2 ounces button mushrooms
1 large egg
1 extra egg yolk
½ cup heavy cream
pepper

Preheat oven to 400°F. Adjust the rack to the center position. Roll out the pastry to line an 8-inch quiche pan. Chill briefly. Line the pastry with greaseproof paper or aluminum foil and fill it with dried beans or ceramic or aluminum pie weights. Bake for 10 minutes. Remove weights and lining and bake for 3 to 5 minutes longer, until pastry is set but not browned.

Trim the chicken livers and sprinkle them with a little salt. Let them stand for a few minutes, then rinse and blot with kitchen paper. Melt the butter in a heavy pan. Add the livers and the Madeira and cook gently for about 10 minutes, until livers are soft but not browned. Lift out livers, reserving the juices from the pan. Chop livers and arrange on the bottom of the pastry. Wipe mushrooms clean, trim stems, and cut caps into thin slices. Set aside.

Beat the whole egg and the extra yolk lightly. Stir in the cream, seasonings to taste, and reserved pan juices. Beat the ingredients together until the custard is blended. Strain the custard into the pastry over the livers. Arrange the mushroom slices decoratively on top.

Bake the quiche for about 25 minutes, until a skewer inserted in the center comes out hot and clean.

Seafood Quiche

8 portions

8 ounces Short-Crust Pastry (see Index)
1 green pepper
4 ounces plum tomatoes
4 ounces fresh mushrooms
1 medium-size onion
1 garlic clove
2 tablespoons unsalted butter
8 ounces shelled raw shrimps
8 ounces fresh mussels in shells
1 can (7 ounces) water-packed tunafish
4 large eggs
½ cup light cream
2 tablespoons tomato purée
salt and pepper
watercress sprigs
1 lemon

Preheat oven to 400°F. Roll out the pastry and line a 10-inch quiche dish. Chill dish and pastry for 30 minutes. Line the pastry with greaseproof paper or aluminum foil and fill with dried beans or ceramic or aluminum pie weights. Bake the pastry for 10 minutes, then remove weights and lining and bake for 3 to 5 minutes longer, until pastry is set but not browned.

Blanch the green pepper in boiling water for 3 minutes; rinse with cold water and drain. Discard stem, ribs and seeds and cut pepper into thin strips. Blanch and peel tomatoes. Halve them and scoop out the juice and seeds from the centers into a sieve set over a bowl. Press juice through the sieve and turn it into a 1-cup measure. Chop the rest of the tomatoes. Wipe mushrooms with a damp cloth, trim the base of the stems, then cut mushrooms into thin slices. Peel the onion and chop it. Peel garlic and put through a press into the onion.

Melt the butter in a skillet and sauté the shelled shrimps over low heat for 2 minutes. Remove shrimps with a slotted spoon. Set aside 8 shrimps for garnish and halve or chop the rest. Place mushrooms, onion and garlic in the same skillet and sauté over medium heat for 5 minutes, until onion is soft. Scrub and debeard the mussels and steam them over 1 inch of water until all the shells open. Remove mussels from shells and add to the shrimps. Discard shells. Filter the mussel liquid through a sieve lined with dampened cheesecloth. Add enough of the strained mussel liquid to the strained tomato juice to fill the measuring cup. Open and drain the tuna.

Reduce oven heat to 375°F. Beat eggs, cream and tomato purée together. Mix in green pepper strips, chopped tomatoes, the mushroom mixture, shrimps, mussels and tuna. Add the cup of mixed liquid and salt and pepper to taste. Spoon mixture into the pastry case. Return to the oven and bake for 40 minutes, or until a knife inserted in the center comes out clean. Let the quiche stand for about 10 minutes before cutting it. Just before serving, garnish with the reserved 8 shrimps, watercress sprigs and lemon wedges. Serve hot or cold.

Fennel and Onion Quiche

4 portions

- **5 ounces Short-Crust Pastry (see Index)**
- **2 onions, each about 2 ounces**
- **1 fennel bulb, about 1 pound**
- **8 ounces plum tomatoes**
- **1 ounce unsalted butter**
- **2 large eggs**
- **½ cup light cream**
- **salt and pepper**
- **pinch of grated nutmeg**

Preheat oven to 400°F. Roll out pastry and line an 8-inch quiche dish. Line pastry with greaseproof paper or aluminum foil and fill with dried beans or ceramic or aluminum pie weights. Bake the pastry for 10 minutes, then remove the weights and lining and bake for 3 to 5 minutes longer, until set but not browned. Set aside.

Peel the onions and chop them fine. Trim the fennel; cut off the stems and remove outer ribs. Cut the tender heart of the fennel bulb into small cubes. Blanch and peel the tomatoes and chop them. Melt the butter in a heavy saucepan over medium heat. Cook the onion until soft and golden. Add fennel cubes and cook until the liquid evaporates, stirring now and then to keep the vegetables from sticking. Add tomatoes and cook until they are soft and mixed with onion and fennel.

Beat eggs and cream together; season to taste. Using a slotted spoon, lift the vegetable mixture from the saucepan, leaving fat and moisture in the pan. Mix the vegetables with the eggs and pour into the pastry case. Return to the oven and bake for 25 minutes, or until the custard is set and the pastry golden brown. Let the quiche set for 10 minutes to make it easier to cut it. Serve warm or cold.

Cheese and Asparagus Quiche

6 to 8 portions

- **6 ounces Short-Crust Pastry (see Index)**
- **3 ounces Stilton or other blue cheese**
- **3 ounces cream cheese**
- **2 large eggs**
- **½ cup light cream**
- **salt**
- **pinch of white pepper**
- **pinch of cayenne pepper**
- **12 cooked fresh asparagus tips**

Preheat oven to 400°F. Adjust rack to the center position. Roll out the pastry to line a 9-inch quiche pan and chill briefly. Line the pastry with greaseproof paper or aluminum foil and fill it with dried beans or with ceramic or aluminum pie weights. Bake for 10 minutes. Remove weights and lining and bake for 3 to 5 minutes longer, until the pastry is set but not browned.

Crumble the Stilton cheese, then mash it with the cream cheese until smooth. Beat the eggs lightly. Stir in the cream and seasonings to taste and beat together until the custard is blended. Strain the custard. Thin the cheeses with a little of the custard, then spread cheese mixture over the bottom of the pastry. Pour remaining custard over the filling. Arrange asparagus tips in the quiche, tips to the outside. If the spears are too long, trim the lower ends to make them fit.

Bake the quiche for about 25 minutes, until a skewer inserted in the center comes out hot and clean.

Soufflé Omelet with Black Currants

2 portions

- **8 ounces black currants or other flavorful berries**
- **3 tablespoons superfine granulated sugar**
- **1 tablespoon crème de cassis (optional)**
- **3 eggs**
- **pinch of salt**
- **1 tablespoon unsalted butter**
- **confectioners' sugar**

Wash the black currants, remove all the little stems, and discard any damaged or unripe berries. Place berries in a pan with 2 tablespoons of the sugar. Crush the currants with a fork, then leave in a cool place for 2 hours so they will release juices.

Cook the currants over medium heat for 8 minutes, shaking the pan from time to time to prevent sticking. If there is not much liquid, add 1 tablespoon cold water or the crème de cassis. Set the cooked currants aside. Preheat oven to 375°F. Butter an 8-inch round gratin dish.

Separate the eggs into 2 clean bowls. Add remaining sugar and 1 tablespoon water to the yolks. Mix until light and creamy. Add the salt to the egg whites and beat with a balloon whisk, a rotary egg beater or an electric mixer until egg whites stand in soft peaks. With a metal spatula, fold the yolks into the whites. Pour the mixture into the buttered dish. Quickly spread it around the dish with a wet palette knife, and make a depression down the center.

Place the gratin dish at the top of the oven and cook for about 7 minutes, until omelet is golden and puffy. Meanwhile heat the broiler to its highest temperature. When omelet is cooked, remove it from the oven. Spoon the black currant filling in the depression. Using a spatula, flip the omelet over to cover the filling. Sprinkle the top with a thick layer of confectioners' sugar. Place under the broiler for about 40 seconds, until the sugar has caramelized.

Variations: This omelet can be made with red currants, mulberries, blueberries, blackberries, and red or black raspberries. Change the liqueur to match the fruit. For a Martinique omelet, replace currants and crème de cassis with banana. Peel and slice the fruit and sauté in butter before spooning the slices into the baked omelet.

Strawberry Soufflé Omelet

2 portions

8 ounces fresh strawberries
2 tablespoons Kirsch liqueur
3 tablespoons superfine granulated sugar, or 1 tablespoon honey
3 large eggs
pinch of salt
1½ tablespoons unsalted butter

Wash and hull the strawberries and set 6 perfect berries aside. Chop the rest and place in a bowl. Sprinkle berries with Kirsch and 2 tablespoons of the sugar. Cover them, and leave in the refrigerator for at least 2 hours.

Separate the eggs into 2 clean bowls. Add remaining sugar and 1 tablespoon water to the yolks. Beat until light and creamy. Add a pinch of salt to the whites. With a balloon whisk, rotary egg beater or electric mixer, beat whites until they stand in soft peaks. Pour the yolk mixture into the whites and fold in with a metal spatula. With a sharp knife, cut the reserved 6 berries lengthwise into halves.

Set the broiler at its highest temperature. Melt the butter in an 8-inch omelet pan over medium heat. Turn the pan so the butter swirls around and coats all sides. When foam has subsided, pour in the eggs. Cook for 1½ to 2 minutes, until the bottom of the omelet is golden, but the top is still runny. Slide the pan under the broiler about 2 inches from the heat source. Cook for 30 seconds, until the omelet has risen and is golden. Make a depression down the center of the omelet. Spoon the chopped berries into the depression; use a slotted spoon so the syrup is not included. Flip half of the omelet over the rest and turn the omelet out onto a warmed plate. Arrange the strawberry halves so they just stick out of the omelet fold. Pour the strawberry and Kirsch syrup around the omelet. Serve at once.

Part Two
ROASTING POULTRY

"Roasting" is a word that has undergone a profound change of meaning in the recent history of cooking. Until perhaps two centuries ago it primarily referred to spit-cooking, in which the food is turned in front of a heat source with free circulation of air over all surfaces. Though few ordinary households had hearths big enough to accommodate great sides or joints of roast meat, many could comfortably roast an occasional chicken or rabbit over the open fire.

Today houses are organized differently, and so are cooking concepts. Every kitchen now possesses an oven, formerly a cumbersome firewood- or coal-hungry structure likely to be maintained only by the village baker or in fairly substantial households. The advent of the home oven meant a revolution in the ordinary household's ability to handle roasting meats. Gradually, oven-baked poultry and meats took on the name of "roasted," while fireplace spit-cooking disappeared and the original concept was slowly forgotten.

The change in meaning is understandable, since oven-cooking has some of the same advantages as spit-cooking. Both are dry-heat methods in which hot air sears the surface of the food to brown it and seal in some of the internal fat and juices. The difference is that air does not circulate as freely around baked food (even when it is placed on a rack), that there is a certain amount of steam trapped in an oven, and that the different surfaces are not equally exposed to the heat. There are ways of getting around the problem—most simply by arranging the food to hang vertically rather than having it lying flat, or by constructing the oven to allow for greater vertical depth so that more convection can be set up by rising hot air. The Chinese are great practitioners of the vertical-roasting approach. Tall deep ovens are used in many parts of the world. Our own ovens are commonly too shallow to hang food, but a vertical roasting stand has recently been introduced, designed to hold a chicken upright during cooking.

In some cuisines, the names of recipes for baked poultry or meat are frequently identified not by any word meaning simply "roasted" or "baked" but by the careful specification "in the oven" or "of the oven"—*tou fournou* in Greek, *al forno* in Italian, *al horno* in Spanish, *au four* in French. The phrase recalls an earlier age when food was taken out to the nearest baker's communal bakehouse. In Greece and some Mediterranean villages this practice was true as recently as 30 years ago.

Because of its extravagant use of fuel, the very idea of the home oven has hardly penetrated Chinese cuisine at all. Poultry, like most meats, is generally cut up into small pieces for stir-frying or other quick brazier-top methods. Instead of communal bread ovens used by individual households, there are professional cookshops and restaurants selling roasted foods from their own ovens. Peking duck—pieces of crispy-glazed duck skin wrapped in small pancakes with duck meat, scallions, and hoisin sauce—is the roasted specialty best known in the West. The skin of the duck is carefully prepared for roasting by being blown up with a bamboo tube or a bicycle pump until it pulls away from the flesh and puffs like a balloon; the duck is then air-dried before roasting. These preliminaries are important because the breed of duck most used in China is very fatty and the skin will remain grease-logged if it is not separated from the flesh. Usually the cavity of the duck is filled with hot water before roasting so that the bird will steam from within and roast from without. To achieve really good results with Peking duck you need an oven high enough for the duck to hang freely, Chinese-style; but it is also possible to place it on a rack.

An extraordinary way of roasting poultry and other meats was developed in northern India. It too is done in a special kind of oven—the *tandoor*—not ordinarily to be found in private homes. Tandoors are large, deep clay ovens sunk into pits. Tandoori chicken, the best-known tandoor specialty, is tenderized with papaya juice, marinated in yogurt and spices, and lowered into the oven on skewers. The preliminary tenderizing and marinating impart a beautifully moist, delicate texture to birds that would otherwise be much tougher than our better-raised chickens. The cooked chicken is marvelously imbued with the earthy quality of the oven and far more succulent than most poultry roasted in a Western home oven—though again, the dish can be recreated with fair success using American appliances.

The American fondness for roast poultry on festive occasions dates back to the days when we too were accustomed to have it cooked outside the home in special ovens. Roast chicken was once Sunday dinner fare (for special Sundays at that); a fine capon was the height of elegance—and is still the paragon of roasting birds. Even when the home oven became an everyday reality, roast chicken long remained something of a luxury. Birds meaty enough to be worth roasting but tender enough to be cooked by oven heat were not taken for granted as unthinkingly even forty years ago as they are today. As a matter of fact, now that we casually apply the name "chicken" to all members of the species, we have forgotten that the word used to refer only to birds far from their full growth; the general word for all representatives of the tribe was "fowl." Now that birds of about two months are the only thing that can usually be seen in the market, it is difficult to appreciate the care that used to go into choosing a roasting bird. A good roasting hen or capon should be mature enough to have real flavor, but not so elderly as to require long hours of stewing.

For larger gatherings it is turkey that has always been the American favorite for roasting. Incidentally, why this bird should rejoice in the name of "turkey" is something of a mystery. On its first arrival in Europe in the sixteenth century, its origins seem to have been quite misunderstood. The Austrians called it "Indian cock" (*Indianicsher Hahn,* later shortened to *Indian*), which sounds correct enough until one realizes that they also called it "Calcutta cock." The French likewise seized on the idea that it was a "chicken of India" (*poulet d'Inde,* later garbled to *dinde*); the English, still more oddly, on the belief that it was a "Turkey cock."

Eventually, the American turkey became much admired in Europe and Brillat-Savarin, the author of *The Physiology of Taste,* wrote that, "the turkey is certainly one of the handsomest gifts the New World made to the Old World . . . [It] is the largest and, if not the most subtle, at least the most tasty of our domestic birds." He called himself, quite unabashedly, a great *dindonophile,* a turkey lover. Another great *dindonophile* was Benjamin Franklin who wrote, "I wish the eagle had not been chosen as the representative of our country. He is a bird of bad moral character . . . The turkey is a much more respectable bird, and withal a true original native of America."

By comparison with chicken and turkey, goose is a very rich meat, self-basted during roasting by the abundant fat under the skin. The tricky part of roasting a goose is to melt off the fat as completely as possible without overcooking the meat. The most common American domestic duck, the so-called Long Island variety, is a descendant of the fatty breed raised in China, and presents the same problems in cooking. Since the bicycle-pump method has never had great currency in the American kitchen, the usual way of coping with the difficulty is to prick the skin of goose or duck all over before roasting to allow as much fat as possible to escape.

Barding is a technique used with many sorts of roast, and—though it is rarely used with turkey today—it is often imperative with some kinds of feathered game. The name comes from the French *barde,* for plate armor, and plate armor is exactly what delicate and very lean birds like grouse or pheasant often need to protect the meat against the dry heat of the oven. For it should be recognized in advance of any cooking adventure that these creatures do not have some of the built-in advantages of birds that have been bred for the table for centuries. The challenge of cooking them is part of their fascination.

The main problem with game is dryness and toughness. In fact, braising or pot-roasting is a safer method for most wild birds—especially larger ones like pheasant and wild turkey—than roasting. But when you are lucky enough to find birds sufficiently mature to be interesting but also sufficiently young enough to be tender, they make excellent roasting. Part of the mystique of game has traditionally been the hanging, or leaving it to age for several days (sometimes as much as two weeks) before cooking. This not only makes the bird easier to pluck, but develops the flavor, though some believe in more development than others. A near-putrid stage of ripeness used to be considered just right; ideas on the subject have become more restrained in recent years.

Small birds, such as the tiny buntings known in France as ortolans, can be eaten whole, including the tiny, fragile bones. Larger birds, despite the care that must be taken in choosing and preparing them for roasting, make a splendid effect when served with the kind of highly savory or fruit-based sauces that are also popular with domestic goose or duck.

For all of the trickiness of handling roast poultry, wild or domestic, the method is peculiarly satisfying. There is something about the sight of a golden bird on a platter that still suggests a Sunday dinner or special company. And even the most ambitious gourmet can never outgrow the pleasures of a bird well and truly roasted—be it a pheasant bagged by the family hunter, a brace of quail from an expensive butcher, or a plain but perfect chicken.

CHICKEN

A perfectly roasted chicken is a simple but real treat—golden crisp skin and juicy meat. But perfect results require time and care.

Roast a fresh chicken within a day or two of purchase since it can easily spoil. To store, unwrap the chicken and remove any giblets from the cavity; store giblets separately for another use. Wrap chicken loosely in plastic wrap or aluminum foil, and place on a plate in the coldest part of the refrigerator.

Frozen chickens should be defrosted in the refrigerator for a day or two, depending on the size of the bird.

Fresh and defrosted chickens should be allowed to come to room temperature for about 30 minutes before roasting.

Rinse the inside and outside of the chicken under cold running water. Drain thoroughly, and pat dry with paper towels. If the skin is left wet, the bird will not brown properly.

Lightly salt and pepper inside of the bird. If you are not going to stuff the bird, place cut pieces of a moisture-producing fruit or vegetable such as an onion, apple, or lemon inside the body cavity to furnish moisture and flavor. Fresh or dried herbs and shallots or garlic, either by themselves or mashed with a walnut-size piece of butter and placed in the cavity, provide additional flavor and the basis for a more savory gravy.

Stuffing a Chicken

1 **Prop chicken up with neck cavity facing upward. Loosely pack stuffing into cavity under neck skin.**

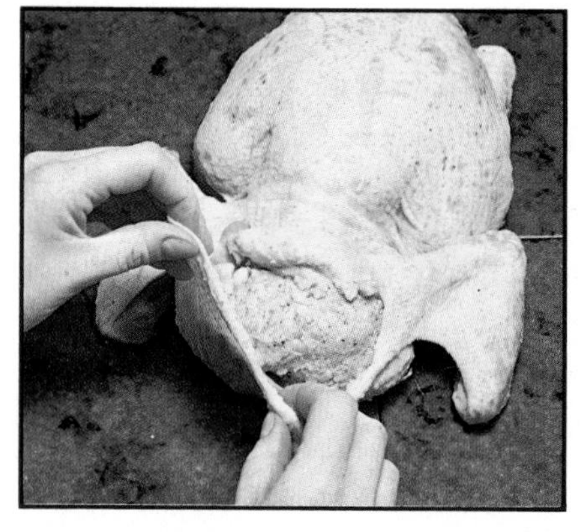

2 **After stuffing, lay bird breast side down. Fold neck skin over stuffing and lay flat across back of bird.**

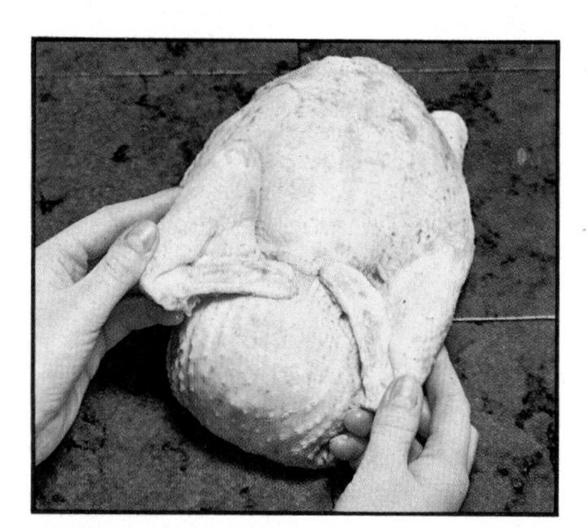

3 **Fold both wing tips over neck skin to secure in place.**

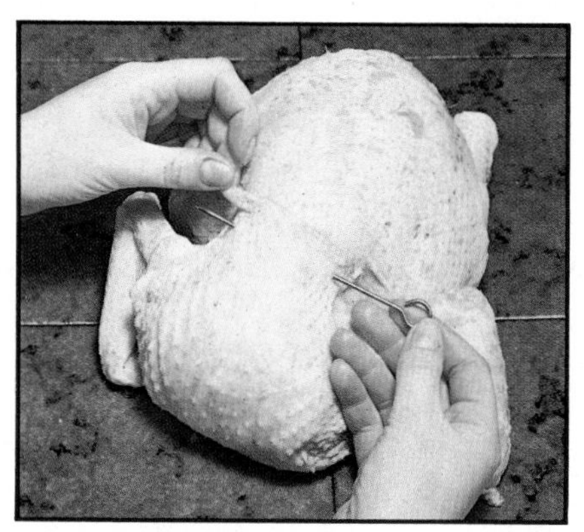

4 **Alternatively, neck skin can be held in place with small poultry skewer. Remove before carving.**

Stuffing and Trussing

Stuffing a bird is another way to add more flavor and moisture. After seasoning, fill the body cavity loosely with stuffing as well as the neck cavity if the large flap of skin is still attached to the neck. Although stuffing can be made ahead, it should not be added until just before roasting. Extra stuffing can be baked in a covered casserole.

Trussing holds the bird in shape during roasting, ensuring even browning. Close the openings with small skewers and a crisscross string. Tie the ends of the drumsticks together and fold the wings back, with the tips under the backbone of the bird. Or use the French method and a trussing needle. Or follow one of the methods in the step-by-step pictures.

Giblets

The giblets, consisting of neck, gizzard, heart and liver, are usually wrapped separately and tucked inside the body cavity. Cut away and discard any green areas from the liver, and remove any thick yellow skin from the gizzard. The giblets, with the liver removed, can be used for making stock. You can also add the cooked heart, gizzard and neck meat, all finely chopped, to the stuffing.

Poultry livers make an excellent filling for an omelet, or for a quiche (see Index for a recipe), and they can be turned into a pâté or used in a terrine. Plan to use poultry livers fresh. They can be frozen, but keep in mind freezing alters the texture.

Poultry livers are not used for stock because they make stock cloudy; also they are tender after brief cooking, while the gizzards and hearts need long simmering to become tender.

Roasting the Bird

Since the breast is the least fatty part of the chicken and is usually exposed to the most direct heat during roasting, use one of these methods to prevent drying of the delicate breast meat:

Bacon. Lay strips of mild-flavored bacon, slightly overlapping, across the breasts and over the tops of the thighs. It may be necessary to replace the bacon strips when roasting a large bird since they may become too crisp. Remove the bacon 20 minutes before the end of roasting in order to let the breast brown.

Covering. Rub the bird with softened butter, and then cover the breast with a buttered piece of heavy-duty aluminum foil or a double thickness of cheesecloth soaked in melted butter. Remove the covering 20 minutes before the end of the roasting time so the breasts can brown.

Rotating. Place a piece of butter and herbs in the cavity of the bird, and rub the outside all over with softened butter. Place the bird directly in the roasting pan, not on a rack, on one side of the breast. Roast for about 25 minutes (15 minutes for small chickens), then shift the bird to the other breast, and baste. After another 25 minutes, turn the bird breast side up, and baste for the final browning. This method takes a bit longer but produces a bird with an all over crisp skin and a succulent breast.

Always preheat the oven: 375°F for a small bird, and 350°F for a larger bird to ensure even cooking all the way through.

If you are cooking the giblets along with the chicken, scatter them in the bottom of the roasting pan underneath the rack and the bird. Roast for 20 minutes per pound for 2½- to 6-pound unstuffed birds. Add 5 minutes per pound for stuffed birds. Baste occasionally with the drippings that accumulate in the bottom of the pan.

The easiest and surest way to judge when the chicken is cooked is to use an instant reading meat thermometer. When inserted in the thickest part of the thigh away from the bone, the meat thermometer should register 180°F.

Alternatively, the juice should run clear or light yellow when the flesh at the thigh joint is pierced with a skewer.

Stuffing Amounts for Poultry

Bird	Weight in pounds	Amount for body cavity	Amount for neck cavity
Cornish game birds	1 to 1½	¼ to ½ cup	1 tablespoon
Broiler or fryer	1½ to 3	1 to 2 cups	¼ cup
Roasting chicken	3 to 5	3 to 5 cups	½ to 1 cup
Capon	4 to 8	5 to 7 cups	1¼ to 1½ cups
Duck	4 to 5	3 to 4 cups	½ cup
Goose	5 to 8	4 to 6 cups	½ cup
	9 to 12	6 to 9 cups	¾ cup
Turkey	9 to 12	4 to 6 cups	1 cup
	15 to 20	8 to 10 cups	1¼ to 1½ cups

Roasting Times for Chicken

Times for roasting fresh birds or fully thawed frozen birds, both at room temperature, stuffed at the neck end only. For birds also stuffed in the body cavity, add an extra 20 to 30 minutes to the time.

Chickens over 6 pounds are usually older birds, which are better cooked by a moist method, such as poaching or braising. All chickens can be roasted at 350°F or 325°F. If you choose a lower temperature, adjust the length of time accordingly.

Weight of oven-ready bird in pounds	Number of servings	Oven temperature	Roasting time
2	2	375°F	50 to 60 minutes
3	4	375°F	1 to 1¼ hours
4	5 or 6	375°F	1½ hours
5	7 or 8	350°F	2 hours
6	8 or 9	350°F	2¼ hours

Serving

Select a serving dish large enough to accommodate all the carved chicken pieces and any garnishes. As you lift the bird from the roasting pan, lift it tail down so excess juices drain into the roasting pan. Let the bird rest for 10 minutes before carving so the juices and flesh will set. Remove trussing strings and skewer. Carving is a relatively simple process once you have mastered the art of finding the ball joint of the thigh.

Roasting Chicken

1 Remove the bird from refrigerator to reach room temperature. Weigh and calculate the cooking time.

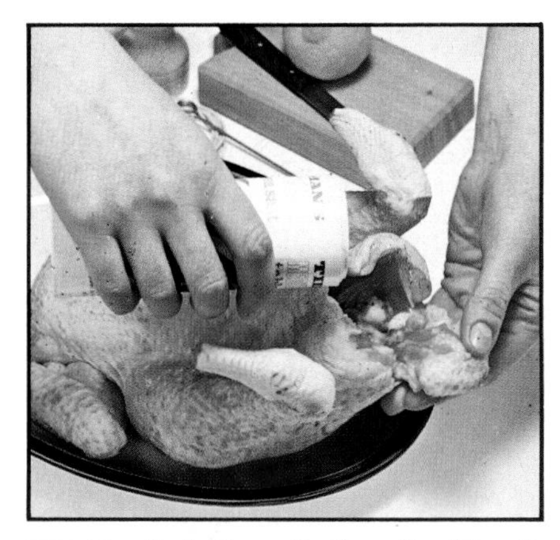

2 Sprinkle cavity liberally with salt and black pepper. Insert stuffing or moisturizing ingredients.

3 Place chicken, breast upwards, on a rack or trivet in a roasting pan.

4 Lay strips of bacon, slightly overlapping, across breast and tops of thighs. Roast the chicken.

5 Remove and discard bacon 20 minutes before end of roasting to allow breast to brown.

6 Baste chicken with accumulated juices from bottom of pan, two or three times during final roasting.

7 Test the chicken by piercing the thigh with a skewer. If the juices run clear the chicken is ready.

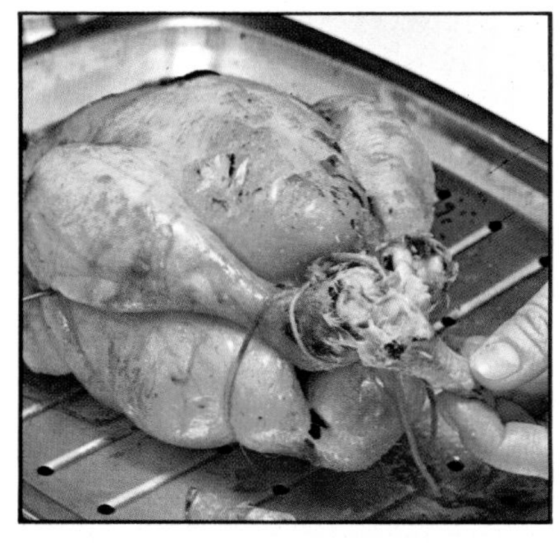

8 Remove any trussing string and the skewers if present.

9 As you lift the bird to transfer it, tilt it so that the juices run from the tail end into the pan.

Carving Large Chicken

- A well-sharpened carving knife and a handle-guarded fork make carving a simple matter.

- Have a long-handled spoon handy for serving the crumbly stuffing.

- A napkin is useful for holding the leg tip when the thigh and drumstick need to be divided.

- Be sure to use a large carving platter to hold all of the meat.

1 Insert carving fork between thigh and rib cage. Remove legs by carving through ball joint connected to body.

2 Hold end of leg with towel and separate leg into thigh and drumstick sections. Repeat with other leg.

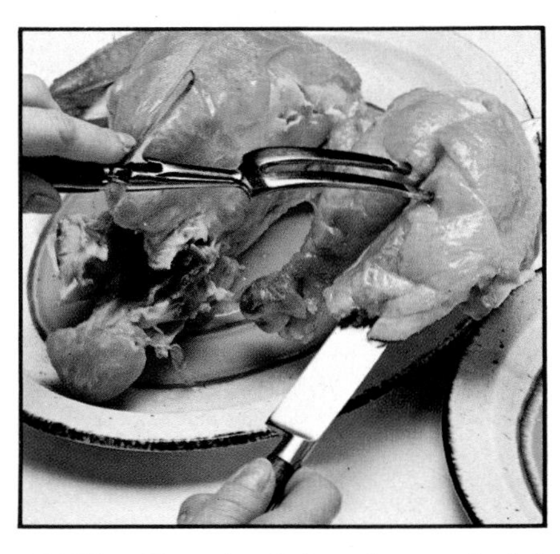

3 Turn the dish and carve the left side.

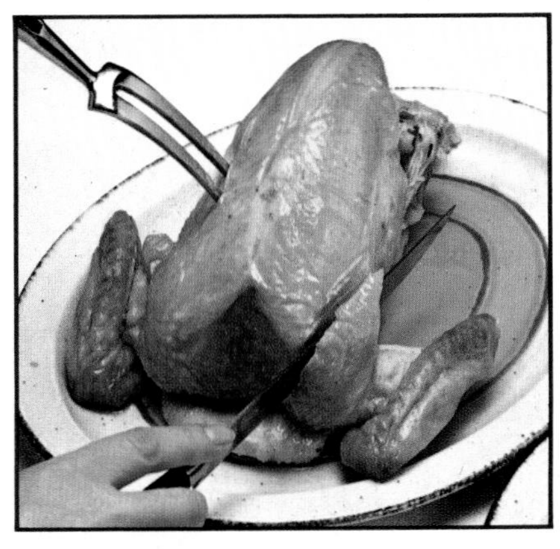

4 Remove wings from breast by cutting through ball joint at base of wing under breast.

5 With wishbone facing right, insert knife at 45 degree angle at end of breastbone.

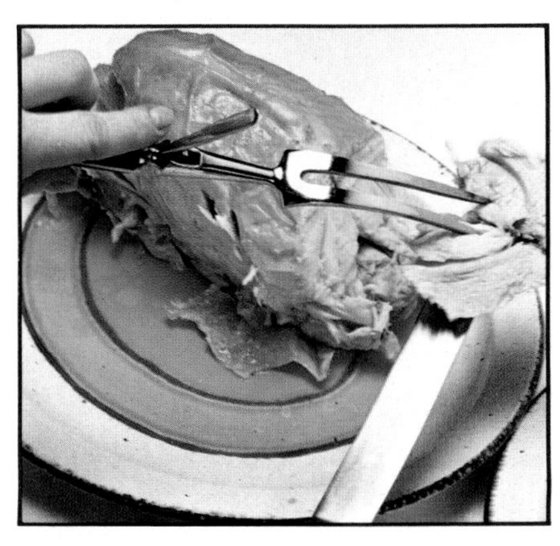

6 Remove wishbone by following curve of bone with knife. Remove bone and attached meat to platter.

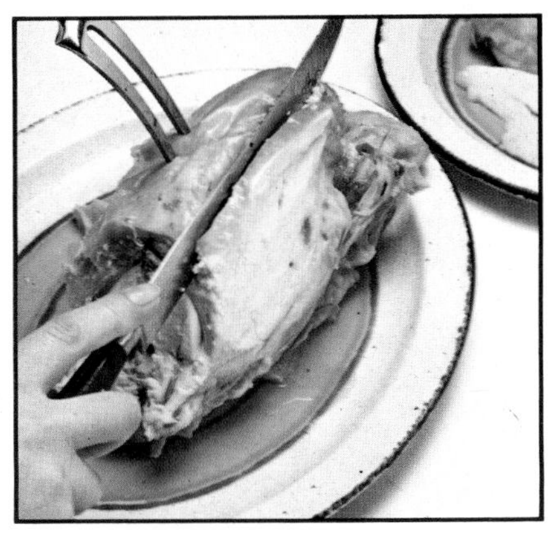

7 With neck end of chicken facing you, carve breast into thin slices holding knife parallel to carcass.

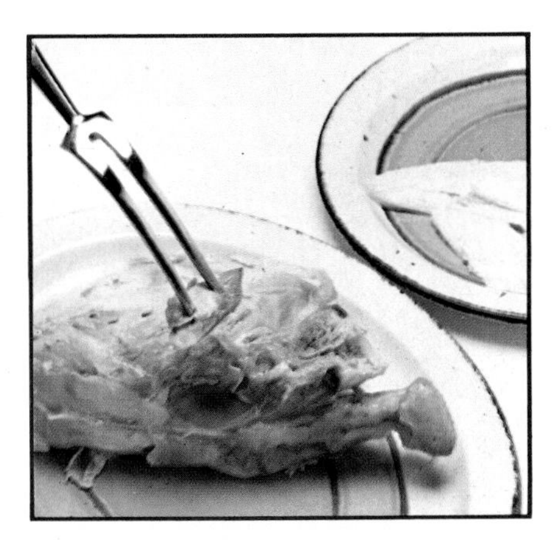

8 Remaining meat such as the oyster pieces on the back can be removed as well.

TURKEY

With the increasing availability of smaller turkeys and turkey pieces, this bird need no longer be only holiday fare, but can become an everyday treat. Choices include fresh-killed turkeys, oven-ready turkeys and frozen turkeys.

When using a frozen bird, remember it requires lengthy thawing. Place the bird, still in its wrapping to prevent drying out, on a rack over a tray or roasting pan to catch the drip; place in the refrigerator. Make sure the bird is thoroughly defrosted before stuffing and roasting. Times will range from 24 to 36 hours for a 5- to 10-pound turkey, to 60 to 72 hours for a 25-pound bird. The defrosted bird should not be kept in the refrigerator for more than 1 day.

Rinse the bird inside and out under cold running water. Drain, and thoroughly pat dry with paper towels. Season the inside with salt and pepper; if there is no stuffing, insert ½ lemon or 1 halved onion, 2 garlic cloves, or a sprig of fresh sage, thyme, basil or marjoram in the body cavity.

The method for stuffing a turkey is the same as a chicken. Loosely pack

Trussing a Turkey

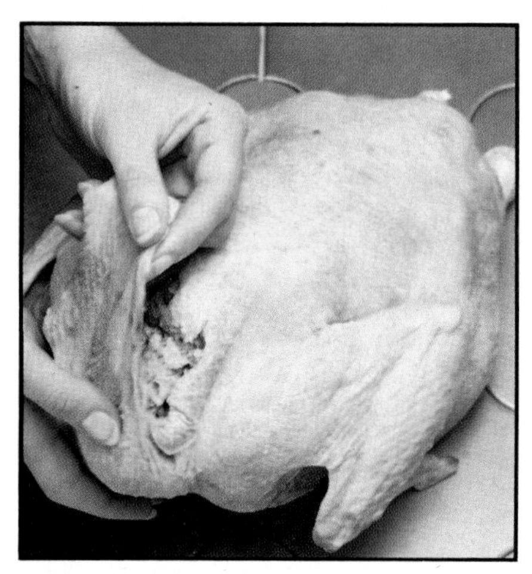

1 Lay turkey breast side down. Make sure neck skin is flat against the back, enclosing any stuffing.

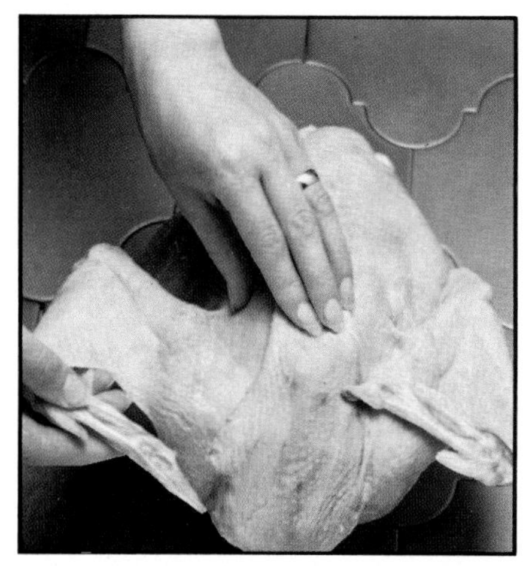

2 Fold wing tips under and across back to hold neck skin in place.

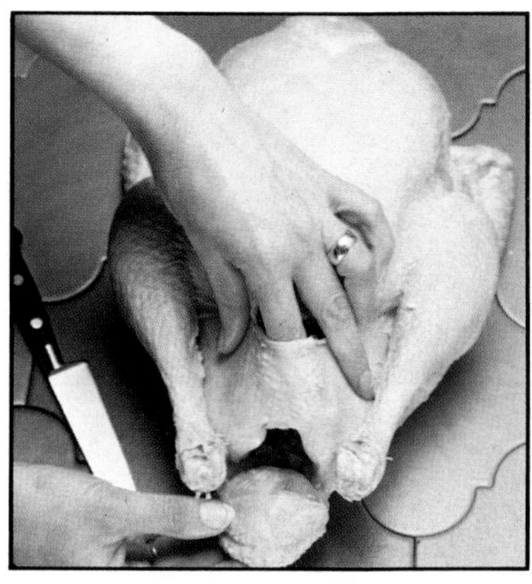

3 Make slit in skin above tail vent and push parson's nose or nub of fat at end of tail through slit.

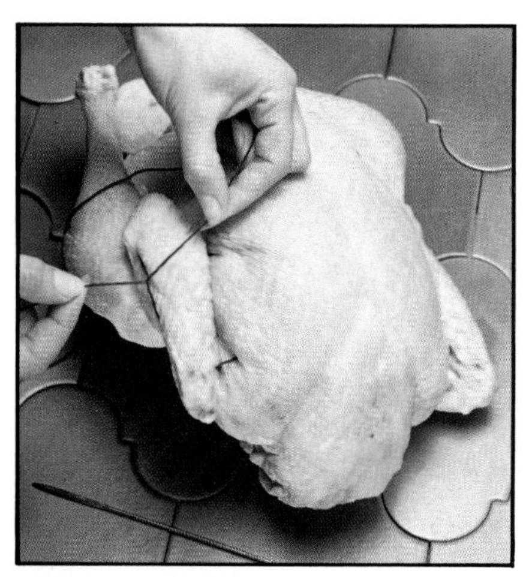

6 Push needle back through body and through first joint of right wing to secure wing tips and neck skin. Tie string securely.

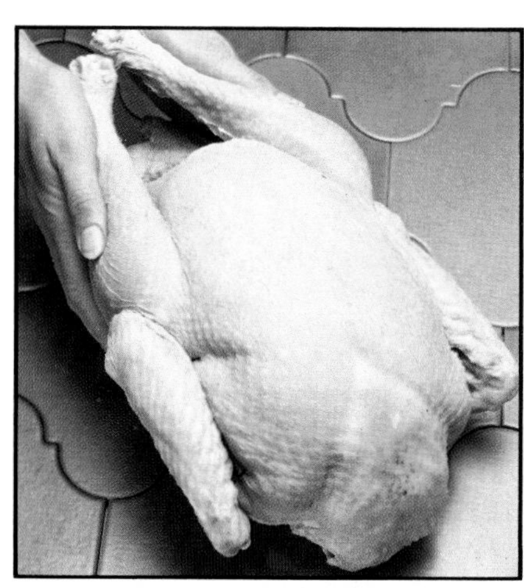

7 Press legs to side of body so breast is plumped up.

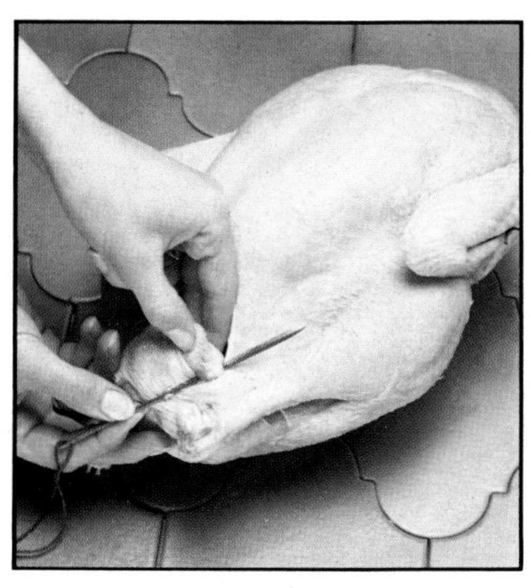

8 Insert rethreaded needle in gristle at right side of tail end. Bring needle through loop to make a stitch.

the neck and body cavities with a moist stuffing just before roasting. The stuffing should be cool. Once the bird has been stuffed, it should be trussed at once. Extra stuffing can be baked in a separate covered casserole for the last 30 to 40 minutes of roasting time.

Trussing a large bird is essential: legs and wings are kept in place and carving is much easier.

A trussing needle works better than a skewer for large birds; use natural rather than a plastic coated or nylon string which will melt during roasting. Look at the step-by-step pictures before you start.

Roasting the Turkey

The methods for roasting large and small birds vary slightly. The times given here are for stuffed birds; for unstuffed turkeys, cook about 5 minutes less per pound.

To prevent drying out, either spread the breast and legs generously with softened or melted butter, or lay strips of bacon over the breast and legs. Replace the bacon as it becomes too crisp during the roasting.

Small turkeys, up to 8 pounds, are best roasted at high heat to ensure the flesh is cooked through but still moist. Place in the center of a preheated 450°F oven. Immediately lower the oven temperature to 350°F, and roast, basting frequently, until an instant reading meat thermometer registers 180°F when inserted in the thickest part of the leg, or the juices run clear when the thickest part of the thigh is pierced with a skewer, 20 to 25 minutes per pound.

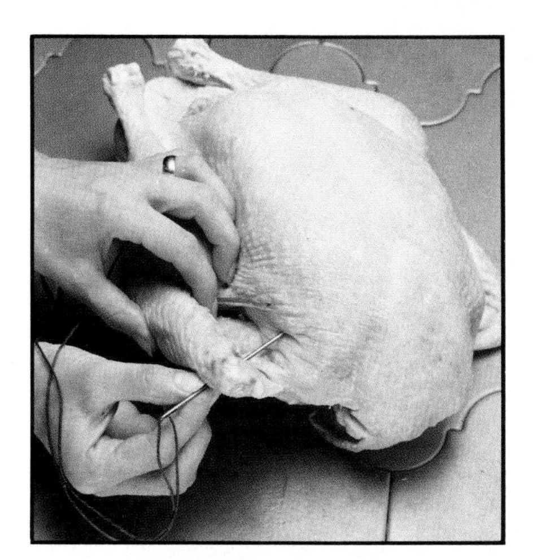

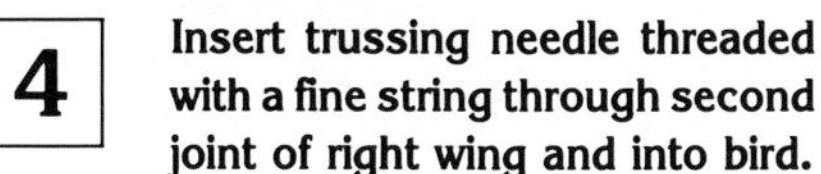

4 **Insert trussing needle threaded with a fine string through second joint of right wing and into bird.**

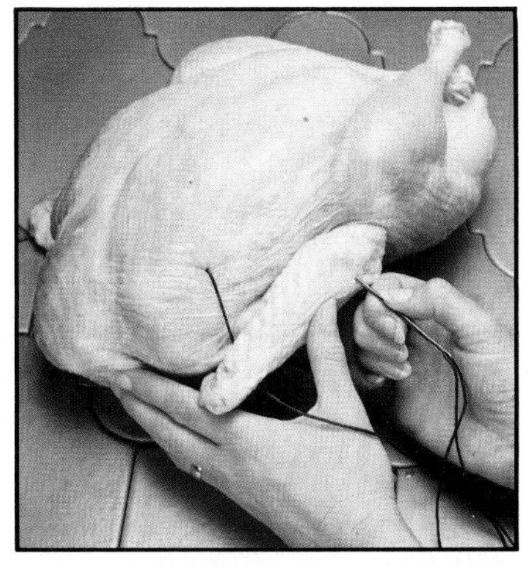

5 **Push needle through body and out through second joint of left wing. Reinsert needle through first joint of left wing.**

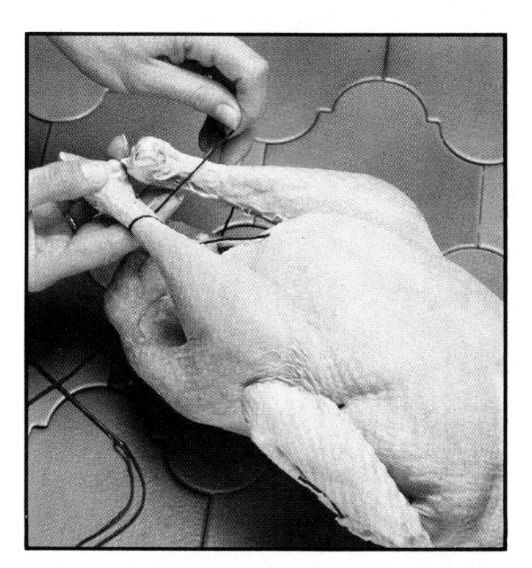

9 **Wrap string around right leg, pass over body, and wrap around left leg.**

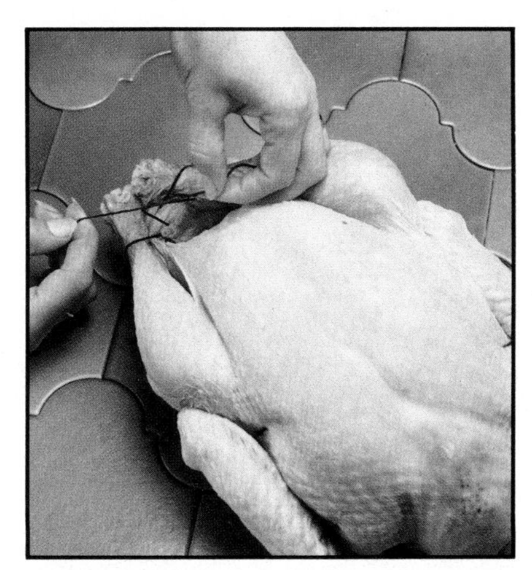

10 **Insert needle in gristle to left of tail vent. Bring string back under nub of tail fat and tie securely.**

Thawing Times for Frozen Turkey

Defrost frozen turkey on a rack set over a tray with sides, in the bottom of the refrigerator. Do not unwrap the bird until it is thawed enough for you to be able to pull out the bag of giblets from the cavity. The bird should be thawed at least 16 hours.

Weight in pounds	Thawing time in hours
5 to 8	20 to 36
8 to 11	36 to 42
11 to 13	42 to 48
13 to 20	48 to 60
20 to 25	60 to 72

Roasting Times for Large Turkeys at 325°F

Weight in pounds	Roasting time in hours
9 to 10	2½ to 3
10 to 12	3½ to 4
12 to 15	4 to 5
15 to 17	5 to 5½
17 to 20	5½ to 6
20 to 25	6 to 7½

Roast large birds at 325°F, basting frequently. Turn the bird every hour to ensure even browning. If using the bacon method, remove the bacon from the breast 20 minutes before the end of the roasting time to allow the breast to brown. If there appears to be overbrowning, cover breast with aluminum foil. Allow 15 to 20 minutes per pound. A large bird should rest for 10 to 20 minutes before carving, to allow the juices and meat to set. If the bird is stuffed, remove the stuffing to a separate bowl and keep warm.

If roasting a turkey to serve cold, cool as rapidly as possible, and then refrigerate, lightly covered, for up to 2 days. Do not cut the meat until necessary as it will dry out quickly.

Duck and Goose

Duck and geese are relished for their pronounced flavor and succulence. They are not, however, fleshy birds, so one duck or goose does not go very far.

Domestic ducks can be purchased in a variety of ways: fresh-killed, fresh oven-ready, and frozen. Select a duck between 3½ and 5 pounds (dressed weight) with a plump breast, creamy white skin and well-rounded legs. A 5-pound bird will serve 4 people. Leftover bones can be used to make stock and soup, and the rendered fat is excellent for frying meat or sautéing or roasting potatoes.

Fresh-killed birds are usually found in live poultry markets in ethnic neighborhoods. A young tender duck will have pale yellow feet and bill, and a bill that is flexible. The birds are plucked but include feet, head and innards, which can increase the oven-ready weight by one third. Refrigerate for no more than 2 days.

Fresh oven-ready ducks are increasingly more available. They are sold either wrapped in plastic in supermarkets, or unwrapped in butcher shops.

Frozen ducks are commonly available in the frozen food sections of some supermarkets and in butcher

Roasting Duck or Goose

1 Rinse bird and pat dry. Prepare required quantity of stuffing. Preheat oven to 425°F.

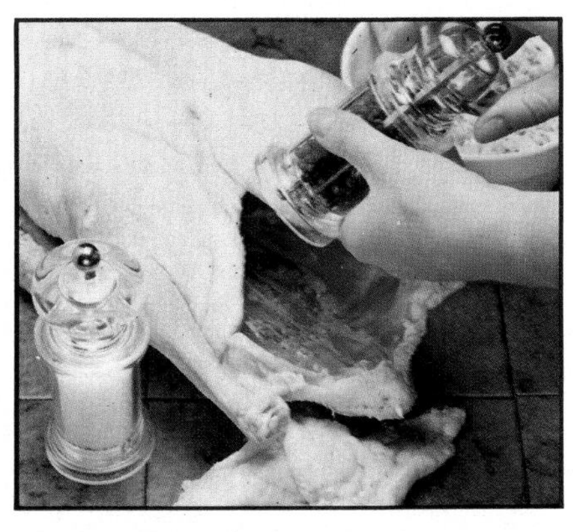

2 Remove solid fat from inside goose. Season inside of the bird with salt and pepper.

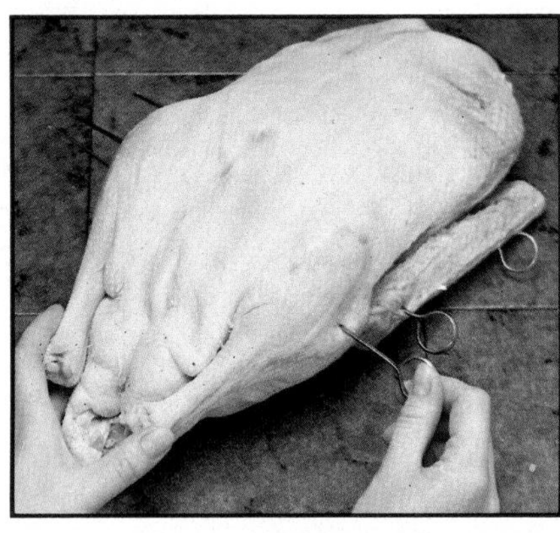

5 Turn the bird onto its back and press the legs to the body. Push the skewer through the thighs.

6 Prick the skin all over to allow fat to escape and rub with salt and freshly ground black pepper.

9 Turn roasting pan so bird browns on all sides.

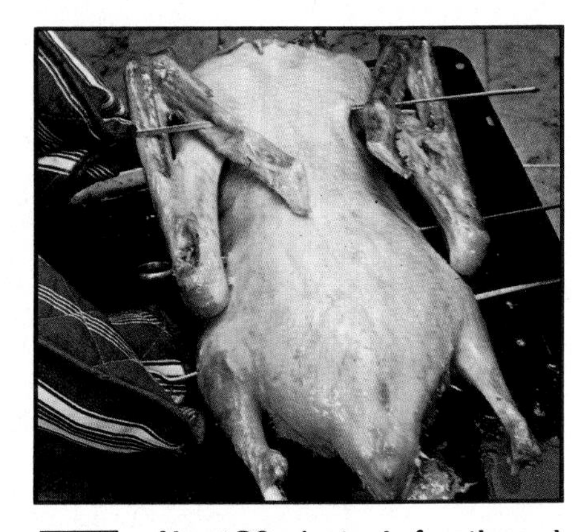

10 About 20 minutes before the end of roasting time, turn bird upside down to brown the back.

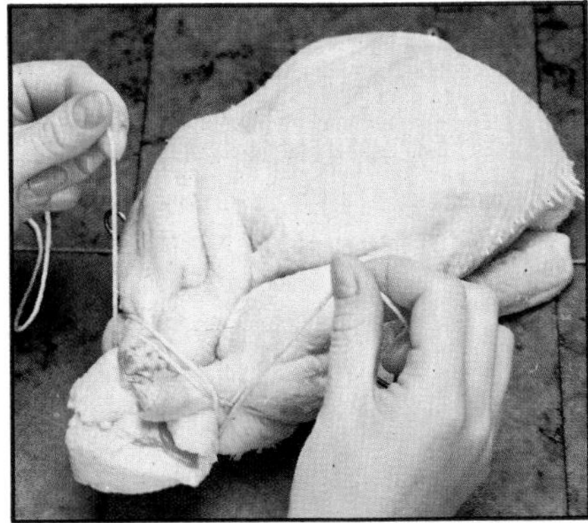
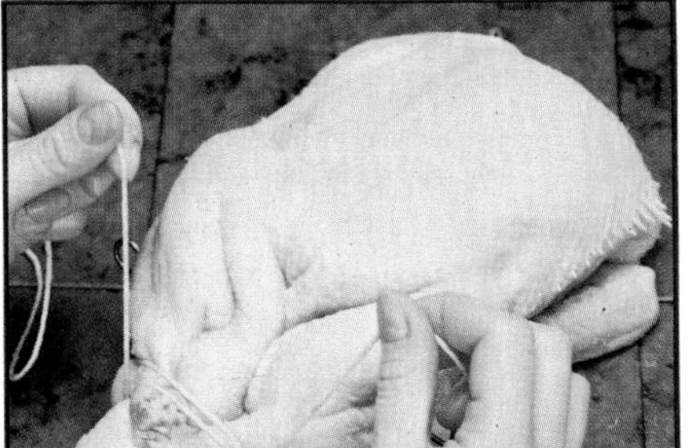

3 Stuff through the tail end. Truss a duck with string in same way as a chicken.

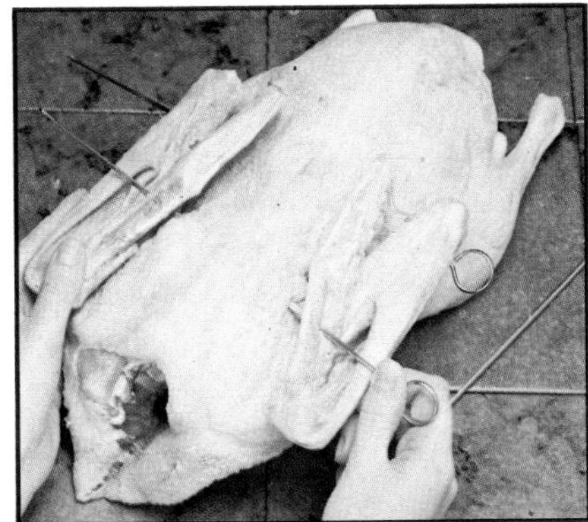
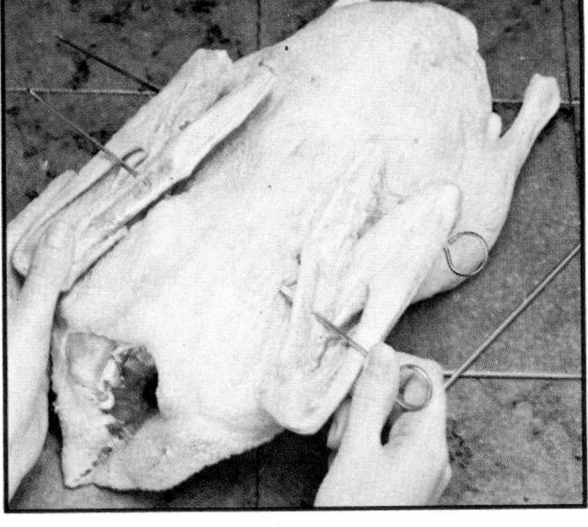

4 A goose can be trussed with 3 skewers. Push one skewer through center joints of wings, one through wing tips.

7 Place bird on rack in roasting pan. Roast in preheated 425°F oven for 15 minutes.

8 Reduce heat accordingly for duck and goose. Roast about 18 minutes per pound. Drain fat from pan at regular intervals.

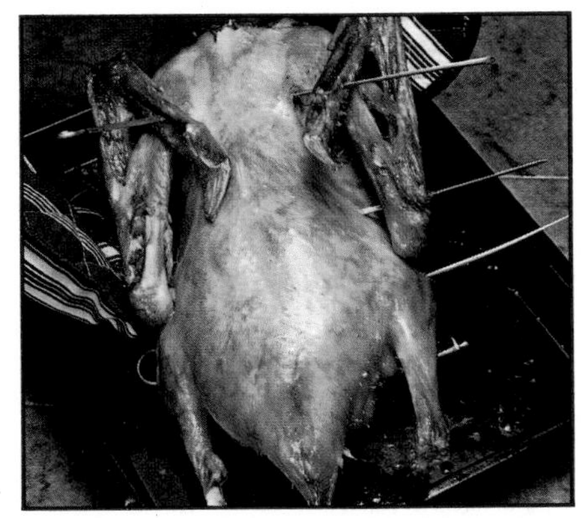

11 Turn breast side up 5 minutes before the end of roasting for a final browning and crisping.

12 To test if cooked, pierce the thick part of the leg with a skewer. The juices should run clear.

shops. Defrost duck in its wrapping on a deep platter in the refrigerator for 1 to 2 days, depending on the size of the bird. Store defrosted duck in the refrigerator for no more than 1 day.

Geese are rarely available fresh killed, or even oven-ready fresh. More commonly available are frozen geese. Defrosting and storing instructions are the same for duck and geese. Defrost in original wrappings on a deep platter in the refrigerator for 1 or 2 days, depending on the size of the bird. Store for no longer than 1 day.

Select a goose in the 6- to 10-pound range; less than 6 pounds will provide more bone than meat, and a bird more than 10 pounds will probably be an older bird with stringy flesh. Remember that with a freshly killed goose, the head, feet and innards are still intact and will account for about half of the weight.

Preparing Ducks and Geese for Roasting

Ducks and geese are handled in a similar fashion. If the bird is frozen, thaw it in its wrapping in the refrigerator for about 2½ hours per pound or until thoroughly defrosted. Remove the large pieces of fat from the body cavity and the neck and tail openings of the bird, and reserve. Rinse the bird inside and out under cold running water, and pat dry with paper towels. Sprinkle the body cavity with salt and freshly ground pepper.

Just before roasting, loosely pack the cavity with the stuffing of your choice. Since the birds contain a layer of fat under the skin, they don't have to be protected during roasting to prevent drying out. Pierce the skin all over with a skewer or fork to help excess fat drain during the roasting.

Ducks and geese can be trussed in the same manner as chickens.

A goose can also be trussed, after stuffing, with 3 skewers. One skewer is pushed through the center joint of one wing and out the other. Pass the second skewer through the wing tips, and the third through the thickest part of one leg and out the other.

Both ducks and geese have excess fat in the body cavity and around the neck and tail, which should be removed before roasting. Cut the fat into small dice and put in a heavy saucepan with about 2 tablespoons of water. Simmer until all the fat is rendered, about 30 minutes. Make sure all the liquid is evaporated, leaving only fat. Strain the fat through a sieve lined with a double thickness of dampened cheesecloth, saving the crisp pieces of fat for flavoring other dishes. Refrigerate or freeze the fat for up to 3 months.

Roasting Duck or Goose

Place the bird, breast side up, on a rack in a roasting pan. Place in the center of a preheated 425°F oven. Roast for 15 minutes to start the fat flowing freely. Reduce the oven temperature to 375°F for goose, and 350°F for a duck. Pour off the fat from the roasting pan and return the pan to the oven, occasionally draining the fat during roasting. If roasting the duck unstuffed, tilt the bird, breast side up, once or twice during the roasting to drain the fat from the body cavity. About 20 minutes before the roasting is completed, turn the bird breast side down on the rack to brown the underside. At 5 minutes before the roasting is completed, turn the bird over to its original position. When done, the internal temperature of the bird should be about 180°F and the juices should run clear when the fleshy part of the thigh is pierced with a skewer. The approximate roasting time for both a duck and a goose is 15 minutes per pound after lowering the oven temperature, and 20 minutes per pound for a stuffed bird.

When roasting is complete, remove trussing strings or skewers and let the bird rest for 10 to 15 minutes to allow juices and meat to set before carving. If the bird has been stuffed, remove the stuffing to a separate bowl and keep warm.

Small ducks, in the 4-pound range, are best cut into 4 serving pieces rather than into smaller pieces and slices. First cut the bird through the breastbone and backbone into halves. Then cut each half into 2 equal serving pieces.

Large ducks and geese should be carved and sliced to facilitate serving. First remove the legs and cut each into thigh and drumstick pieces. Cut away the wing, with a little breast meat attached. Slice the breast into vertical slices while still attached to the bone. Free the breast slices by cutting along the rib cage.

Accompaniments

A giblet gravy, with the addition of a little port or orange juice, is delicious with either duck or goose. To provide additional flavor for the pan gravy, place sliced crab apples or regular cooking apples in the roasting pan beneath the bird.

Red currant jam or jelly as a condiment offsets the richness of the birds.

Sliced oranges and bunches of watercress are always an attractive garnish.

Portioning Duck

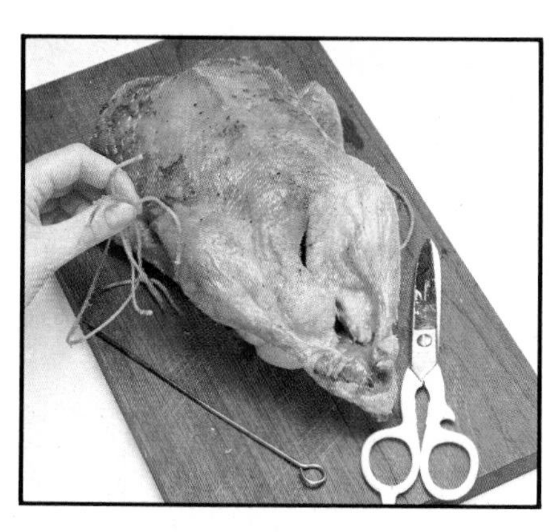

1 **Allow duck to rest for 10 to 15 minutes before cutting. Remove skewer and trussing string from duck.**

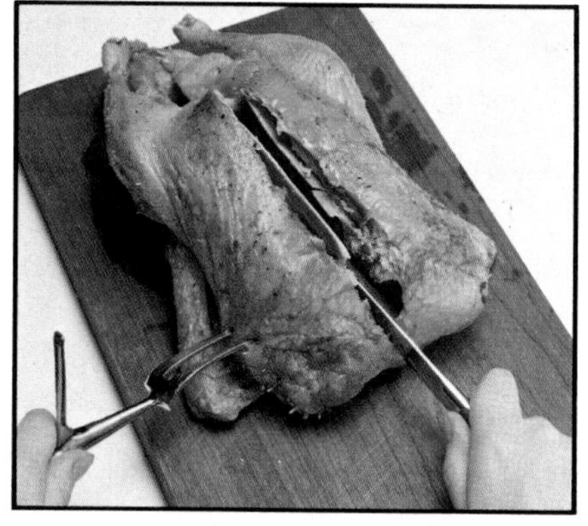

2 **With a sharp heavy knife cut duck into halves, first through breastbone, then through backbone.**

3 **Cut each half into 2 pieces by cutting diagonally through carcass just above thigh, leaving some breast meat attached.**

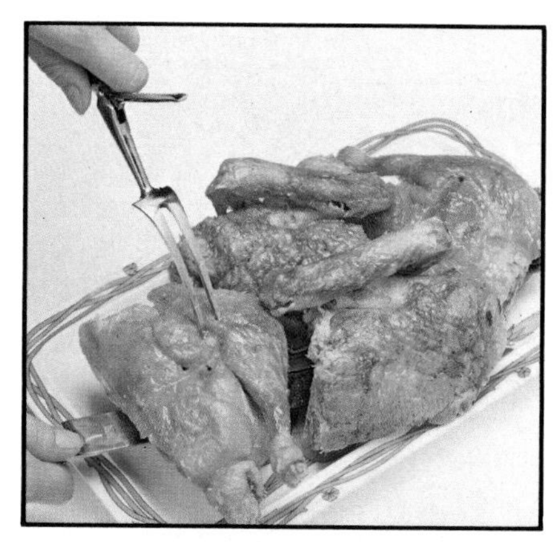

4 **Trim duck pieces of excess fat. Remove bone if necessary. Return to oven to reheat if there is a delay in serving.**

Vegetables should be kept simple, allowing the bird to be the main attraction. Julienned potatoes, grilled tomatoes, peas, or boiled new potatoes are just a few of the possibilities.

Cooked fruit is a welcomed addition—oranges, apples, cherries, peaches, among others.

GAME BIRDS

Game, when it comes to birds, generally means those which are hunted as sport. Wild duck and geese, partridge, quail, pheasant and pigeon or squab are the most commonly hunted game birds.

Most game birds benefit from a period of hanging in the open air after shooting; the flavor improves and the flesh becomes more tender. The innards are removed, which is frequently not the case in Europe, and the bird is hung with feathers, head and feet attached. A bird will be hung from 2 to 10 days, depending on the size of the bird and the weather, colder weather requiring longer hanging, until the tail feathers can be easily plucked out.

Some birds, notably quail and pheasant, are frequently raised on game farms, and sold either fresh or frozen to butchers or live poultry markets. Bought fresh game birds will usually be plucked and cleaned, but ask whether additional hanging time is needed. Frozen birds need to be slowly defrosted in the refrigerator and used within 1 day of defrosting.

Select young birds for roasting since their meat is more tender. Look for soft, pliable feet, a flexible breastbone, yellow, not dark legs and white fat. Older birds are suitable for soups and stews. If the bird still has its plumage, deduct 50 percent of the total weight for a large bird, and 35 percent for a smaller bird, to calculate oven-ready weight.

Some of the most popular game birds include the following:

Partridge. Wild partridge should be hung for 3 to 5 days. Domestic partridge raised on game farms are available most of the year. The bird is also now available frozen. One partridge makes 1 or 2 servings, depending on size.

Pheasant. Large pheasants should be hung for 3 to 5 days. Some are raised on game farms for markets specializing in game. Look for short, rounded claws in the young pheasant, and longer, sharper ones in older birds. One pheasant serves 2 to 3 people.

Quail. In addition to the many varities of wild quail, there are domestic birds available in some areas. Usually 2 quail make 1 serving.

Squab or Pigeon. These birds have a distinctive but delicate flavor, and range from ¾ to 1¼ pounds. Count on 1 bird per serving.

Wild Ducks. Mallard and Muscovy ducks are sometimes found in live poultry markets or Chinese markets. If killed in the wild, hang for 3 days. Wild duck is better braised, although some prefer to slow-roast a stuffed wild duck.

Cornish Game Hen. This is a cross between a chicken and a squab and weighs on the average between 1 and 2 pounds. Its mild taste is more like chicken than like game. Count on 1 bird per serving.

Preparing Game Birds for Roasting

After hanging for the appropriate period of time, the bird is plucked and rinsed inside and out under cold running water, then thoroughly dried. Since game birds tend to be dry, a rich stuffing will add moisture. The bird should be stuffed just before roasting with a cool stuffing. Cavity openings can be closed after stuffing with thin poultry skewers. A walnut-size piece of butter, flavored with lemon or orange juice, or watercress, can be substituted for a stuffing. The bird is trussed in the same manner as a chicken.

To prevent the bird from drying out during roasting, wrap a sheet of pork fat or thin strips of bacon around the breast and legs of the bird, and secure with string. In the case of quail, the entire bird is often wrapped in a thin sheet of pork fat. (This wrapping is called "barding.")

Roasting Game Birds

Preheat the oven to 450°F; a quick roasting at a high temperature helps to prevent drying. Generously butter a roasting pan large enough to hold the bird snugly. Place the prepared bird on a rack in the pan and roast until the juices run clear when the thickest part of the thigh away from the bone is pierced. This will take about 20 minutes per pound. Remove the larding 10 minutes before the end of the roasting time to allow the bird to brown. The breast can be lightly floured before the last 10 minutes of roasting to form a crust, if desired.

Since small game birds serve 1 to 2 people, they are served whole or split into halves by cutting down through the breastbone and then chopping through the backbone with a cleaver. Birds in the 3- to 5-pound range can be carved in the same manner as a small chicken.

A very attractive way to serve roast game birds is on toasted or sautéed good-quality white bread. These finished pieces are called croûres (crusts).

Remove the crusts from a thick slice of bread. Toast, or sauté in butter, until pale golden. The toast then goes under the rack and juices from the bird drip down on to it.

Roasting Game Bird

• Be sure to let the bird or birds rest for about 10 minutes before carving.

• The robust flavors of wild rice or buckwheat groats make these unusual grains perfect choices for stuffing game birds.

1 Loosely fill the body cavity with prepared stuffing.

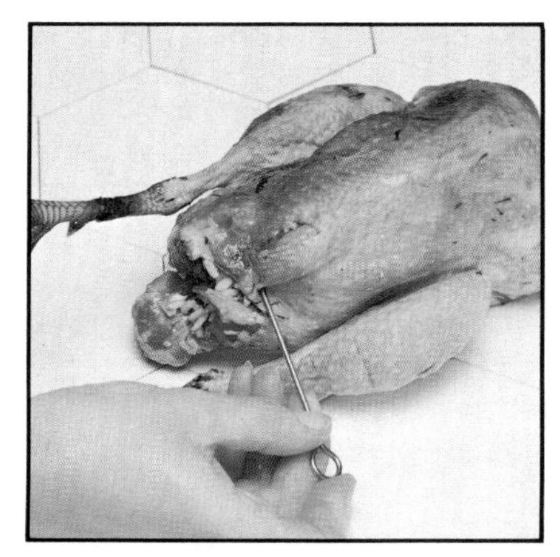

2 Close the cavity opening with thin poultry skewers.

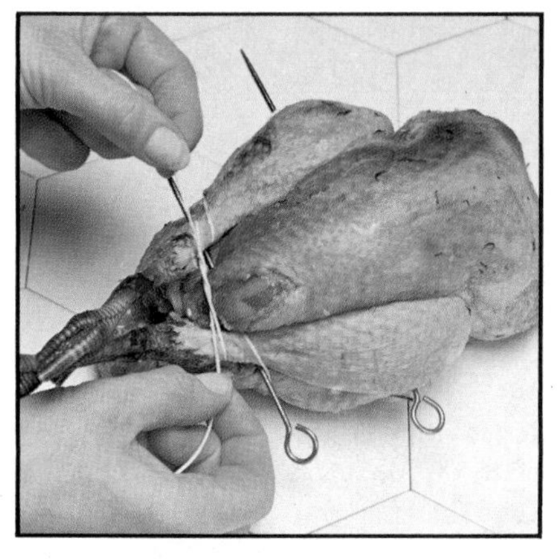

3 Truss according to directions for trussing a chicken.

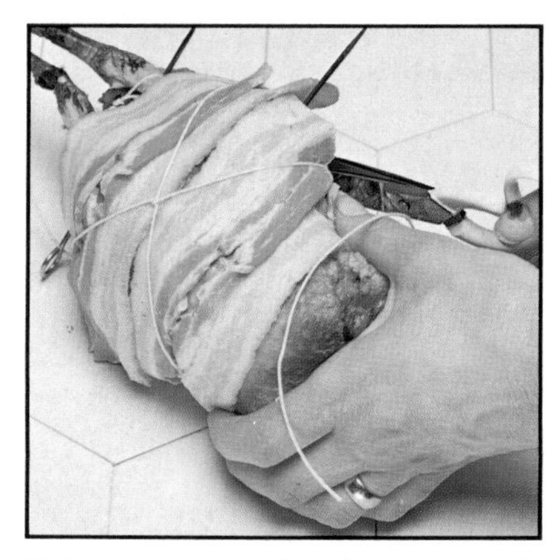

4 Tie thin strips of bacon or pork fat over breast and legs.

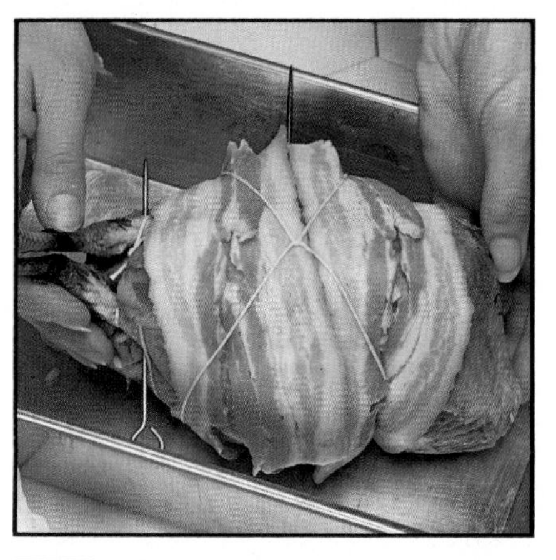

5 Generously butter a roasting pan, large enough to hold bird or birds snugly.

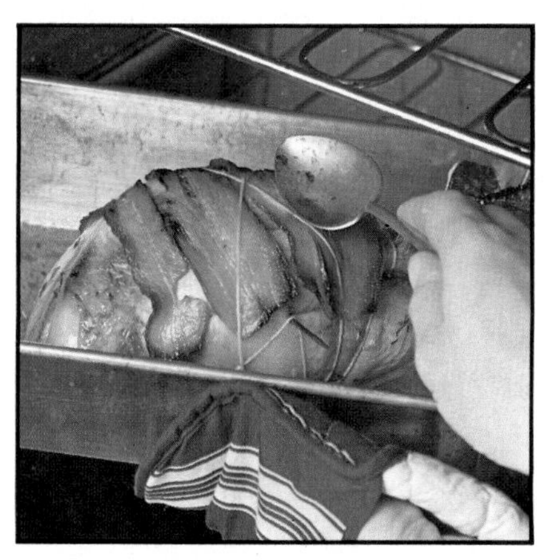

6 Roast bird in center of oven until juices run clear when the thigh is pierced. The time depends on kind and weight of the game bird.

7 Ten minutes before the end of the roasting time, remove strings and bacon from bird.

8 Return bird to oven, sprinkling with flour for a crust, if desired, to allow breast to brown.

Canard à l'Orange (Roast Duck with Orange Sauce)

Canard à l'Orange (Roast Duck with Orange Sauce) (continued)

2 portions

- 1 oven-ready duck, 3 pounds
- salt and pepper
- 4 thin-skinned oranges
- 2 tablespoons sugar
- 1/4 cup red-wine vinegar
- 1 cup Giblet Stock (see Index)
- 1 teaspoon arrowroot
- 3/4 cup port wine
- 1 lemon
- 3 tablespoons orange-flavored liqueur or orange juice
- 2 tablespoons butter

The classic *canard à l'orange* is a favorite restaurant dish that is actually simple enough to prepare at home. The sauce, based on giblet stock made with duck giblets, can be made in advance and reheated.

Serve the duck with red wine and accompany with wild rice or sautéed potatoes.

- Traditionally the sauce is made with bitter Seville oranges. If you can find them, usually in winter, they will make a delicious sauce. If you cannot find them, use good oranges and add a little lemon juice.

- Peel the rind of the oranges with a vegetable peeler or a zester or a sharp paring knife. Do not include any of the white part of the peel when removing the rind.

- Blanching the strips of rind first will remove all traces of bitterness.

- The vinegar-based caramel adds a deep rich color and delicious taste to the sauce.

- For a smooth sauce, blend the arrowroot with cold port and warm the mixture before adding it to the hot sauce.

- When reducing the pan juices, be sure to scrape up any browned bits in the roasting pan for they will provide added duck flavor.

- For a glossy finish, add the butter to the sauce off the heat.

- Serve the sauce warm in a warmed sauceboat.

- Garnish the duck with the half slices of orange.

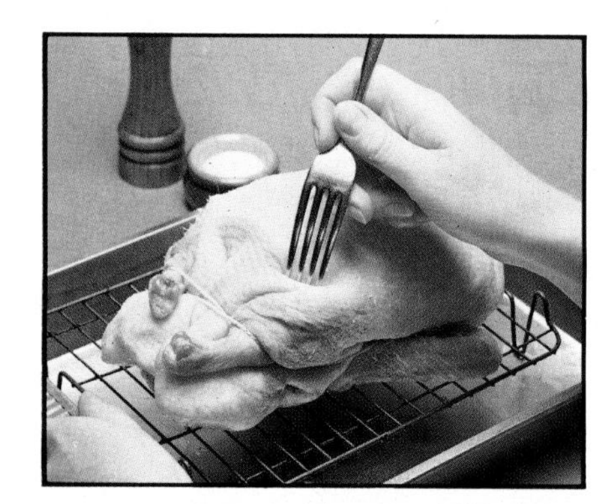

1 Preheat oven to 425°F. Sprinkle inside of duck with salt and pepper. Truss duck. Pierce skin all over with a fork to release fat. Roast for 1½ to 2 hours.

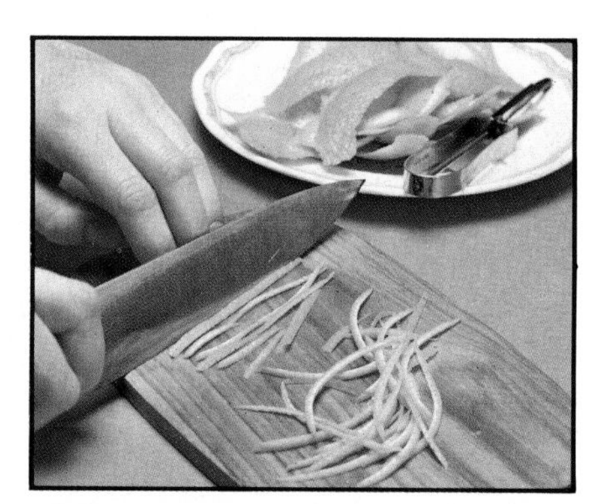

2 Meanwhile, peel 2 oranges with a vegetable peeler or zester. Cut the rind into julienne strips.

3 Place rind strips in a pan and cover with water. Bring to a boil. Simmer for 5 minutes. Drain well.

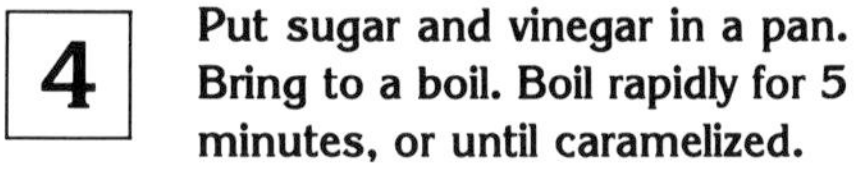

4 Put sugar and vinegar in a pan. Bring to a boil. Boil rapidly for 5 minutes, or until caramelized.

5 Remove caramel from heat and add half of stock. Stir over low heat to release caramel from pan.

6 Add remaining stock to caramel, bring to a boil, reduce heat again, and simmer for 2 minutes.

7 Blend arrowroot with 2 tablespoons cold port. Add a little of the hot sauce and blend well.

8 Stir thickening into sauce. Add reserved orange rind and lemon juice to taste. Simmer for 3 minutes and set aside.

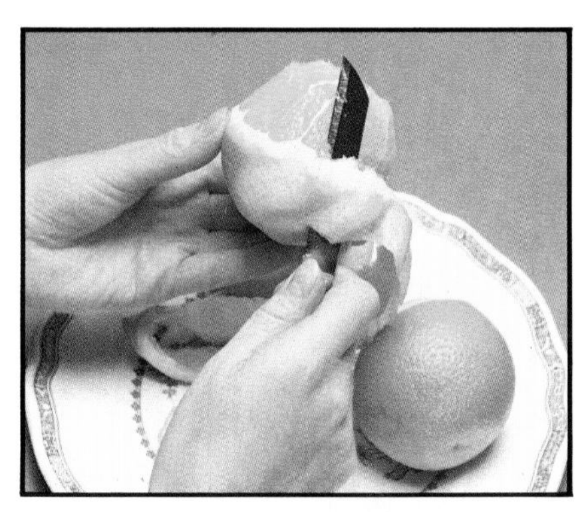

9 Slice ½ orange for garnish. Peel the other oranges, remove white pith, and separate oranges into segments.

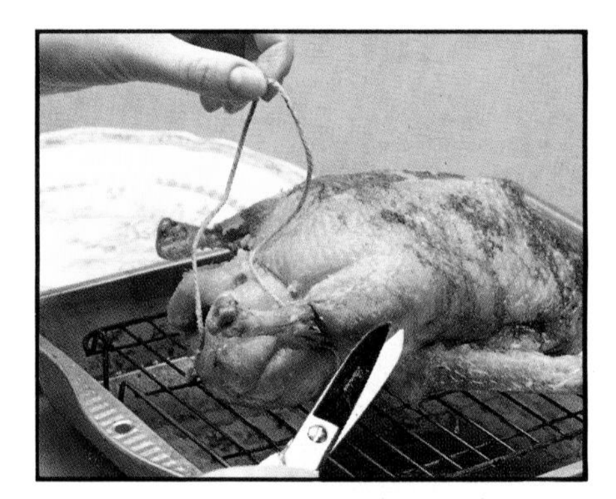

10 Remove cooked duck from oven. Remove trussing strings. Keep warm on a serving place. Surround with orange segments.

11 Tip fat from roasting pan. Add remaining port. Boil, stirring, until reduced to 3 tablespoons.

12 Warm sauce over low heat. Strain in port reduction and simmer. Stir in liqueur and butter.

Roast Duck with Walnut Sauce

4 portions

- **1 oven-ready duck, 5 pounds**
- **salt and pepper**
- **2 ounces fresh brown bread crumbs**
- **1 celery rib**
- **1 small onion**
- **1 orange**
- **1 lemon**
- **1 large egg**
- **2 red-skinned apples (Winesap)**
- **1 bunch of watercress**

Walnut Sauce

- **1 cup Giblet Stock (see Index), made with duck giblets**
- **2 shallots**
- **4 ounces shelled walnut halves**
- **1 teaspoon flour**
- **½ lemon**
- **½ cup sweet sherry**

Prepare the duck for stuffing. Preheat oven to 425°F. Sprinkle the cavity of the duck with salt and pepper.

Make the stuffing: Place the bread crumbs in a bowl. Trim and chop the celery; peel and chop the onion. Grate the rind from the orange and lemon and squeeze the juice from both. Add all these ingredients to the bread crumbs. Break the egg into the bowl and mix well to bind the mixture. Stuff the duck and sew the opening or skewer it closed. Truss the duck, and place it on a rack in the roasting pan. Prick the skin all over with a fork. Roast the duck for 18 minutes per pound of duck and stuffing. As the duck cooks, drain off the fat from the pan or draw it off with a bulb baster. Reserve the fat.

When the duck is cooked, transfer it to a warmed serving platter and keep it warm. Pour off the fat from the roasting pan and set it aside. Add ½ cup of the giblet stock to the pan juices. Place 3 tablespoons of the duck fat in a heavy pan. Peel and chop the shallots and add to the pan with the walnuts. Sauté over medium heat for 2 minutes, then remove from the heat and stir in the flour. Return to heat and cook for 1 minute. Again remove the pan from heat and stir in remaining giblet stock. Return pan to heat and simmer for 5 minutes, stirring all the time, until the mixture is thick. Squeeze the juice of the lemon into the sauce and add the sherry. Stir, then pour the sauce mixture into the roasting pan. Simmer the mixture over low heat, scraping and stirring to release all the baked-on duck juices and deglaze the pan. Strain the sauce and return to the heat to keep it warm.

Peel and core the apples and cut into rings. Sauté the rings in some of the reserved duck fat for about 2 minutes on each side, until apples are golden. Portion the duck and garnish with the apple rings and watercress sprigs. Divide the stuffing also. Spoon a little of the sauce over the apples and portions of stuffing and serve the rest in a sauceboat.

Roast Quails with Brandy

4 portions

- **8 quails**
- **1 lemon**
- **½ cup all-purpose flour**
- **1 teaspoon salt**
- **¼ teaspoon black pepper**
- **¼ teaspoon grated nutmeg**
- **4 ounces unsalted butter**
- **3 ounces brandy**

Preheat oven to 375°F. Rinse quails inside and out and dry thoroughly. Halve the lemon and remove seeds. Squeeze lemon juice on the quails, inside and out. Mix flour, salt, pepper and nutmeg; sprinkle evenly over the birds. Melt the butter in an ovenproof skillet over medium heat. Add the quails and sauté them, turning to brown evenly on all sides. Place the skillet in the oven and roast quails for 20 to 25 minutes, basting frequently, until they are tender. The juices should run clear when the breast is pierced with a skewer.

Transfer quails to a warmed heatproof platter. Heat the brandy, pour it over the quails, and ignite it. When flames subside, pour pan drippings over the birds and serve at once, 2 quails for each portion.

Golden Cornish Hens

4 portions

- **4 Cornish hens, 1 pound each**
- **salt and pepper**
- **2 large oranges**
- **2 bay leaves**
- **3 ounces butter**
- **1¼ cups orange marmalade**
- **watercress sprigs**

If the hens are frozen, let them defrost completely. Preheat oven to 375°F.

Remove the packets of giblets from the birds and set them aside for another use. Rinse the birds inside and out and sprinkle the cavities with salt and pepper. Peel and section the oranges and divide the sections among the 4 birds. Add ½ bay leaf to each bird. Close the cavities and fasten with a small skewer. Tie the legs together. Melt the butter. With a pastry brush coat the birds all over. Set them in a roasting pan large enough to hold them without crowding, and put them in the oven.

As the birds start to cook, heat the marmalade in a small heavy saucepan until it is liquefied. Then strain it to remove the pieces of rind. Return marmalade to the saucepan and stir in remaining melted butter. Keep this mixture warm but do not let it cook. Every 10 minutes, brush the birds with some of the mixture until they are golden and glazed, and done to your taste, about 1 hour. Transfer the birds to a serving platter and decorate with watercress sprigs. Wild rice is a perfect accompaniment for the orange-flavored birds.

Roast Pheasant with Red Wine

4 portions

- **1 pheasant, about 3 pounds**
- **2 Greening apples**
- **1 large onion, 5 ounces**
- **3 celery ribs with leaves**
- **1 large bay leaf**
- **½ teaspoon salt**
- **2 peppercorns**
- **2 coriander berries**
- **6 tablespoons corn oil**
- **2 ounces brandy**
- **4 slices of bacon**
- **2 cups red Bordeaux wine**
- **½ cup red currant jelly**
- **grated rind of 2 oranges**

Dress the pheasant. Rinse inside and out and dry thoroughly. Preheat oven to 400°F.

Wash and core apples; do not peel them. Chop apples. Peel and chop onion. Trim and chop celery. Break bay leaf into bits. Put all these ingredients into a large bowl and sprinkle with the salt. In a mortar crush peppercorns and coriander berries and add to the apple mixture. Stir well. Put the mixture into the cavity of the pheasant and sew the opening or close it with skewers. (The stuffing is used for flavoring and will be discarded when the bird is done.) Truss the bird.

Heat the corn oil in a heavy skillet large enough to hold the bird and in it brown the bird on all sides. Heat the brandy, pour it over the bird, and ignite it. (Flaming game birds helps to modify any gamey taste.)

Transfer the pheasant to a roasting pan. Arrange 3 bacon slices over the breast; halve the remaining slice and place 1 piece on each leg joint. Roast the bird at 400°F for 20 minutes, then reduce heat to 325°F and roast uncovered for about 1½ hours longer, or until done to your taste. After the first hour, baste the bird with red wine every 10 minutes. When all the wine is used, baste with the pan drippings. About 20 minutes before the bird is done, remove the bacon pieces to let the breast and legs finish browning.

Lift the pheasant to a plate and remove trussing strings and threads or skewers. Pour out the stuffing mixture and discard it (the apple and vegetables will be mushy). Skim fat from the pan juices and stir in currant jelly and orange rind. Thicken the gravy if you like, or fluff in a little butter.

Serve the pheasant whole, to be carved at table, or carve before serving.

Part Three

SAUTÉING AND STIR-FRYING VEGETABLES

It is fascinating to explore how various foods and cooking procedures have acquired their names.

Stir-fry in Chinese is *chao* (or *chow*). Written in Chinese, the name includes part of the character which indicates "fire," and part of the character indicating "a little bit." While these ideas are not the precise origins of the term *chao,* the term does suggest the overall concept of "cooking briefly over fire." Certainly one of the main advantages of cooking vegetables by stir-frying them in a wok is that the total cooking time is very brief indeed—not longer than 10 minutes and often less than 5. For the Chinese, who invented it, this was crucial because cooking fuel was a scarce and precious commodity. Today, in America, we may be less concerned with conservation, but the brief cooking time is still important because we want to retain the nutrients as well as the flavor, texture and color of fresh vegetables.

The term *stir-fry* was probably unheard of in this country, as recently as 20 years ago, by all but a few serious aficionados of Chinese cooking. Actually, even this term can be misleading because, if the foods are to cook through quickly and evenly, they are not exactly stirred, but must be tossed constantly over the entire surface area of the pan. In *James Beard's American Cookery,* he says admiringly that, "Apart from the great organic kick, the most notable recent development in vegetables has been the interest in 'stir-fry' cookery, an outgrowth of the popularity of Chinese food. This quick, efficient method of treating vegetables may help their cause immeasurably. After our experience with over-cooked, greasy vegetables, stale vegetables, over-refrigerated vegetables, stir-frying may revive the demand for fine, flavorful, crisp vegetables in their prime."

You will hardly find a modern cookbook today that does not include the versatile technique of stir-frying. The origins may be Oriental and the technique associated with the flavorings of Chinese food, but increasingly you will find more and more Western recipes adapted to the stir-fry method of cooking.

The stir-fry is based on the principle of complementary flavors and textures, often featuring delicate plays of contrasts: large and small ingredients, blends of different colors, bland and hot flavors, and opposing textures such as *tsuei* (crunchy) and *nun* (soft and tender).

In stir-frying, various ingredients that have been cut into small pieces are tossed in a small amount of very hot fat, over a large surface area. The best cooking utensil for this is the *wok,* or *wo* (a closer approximation of the Chinese sound). The procedure, which allows food to be cooked very quickly, brings out fresh flavors, crisp textures, and bright colors optimally, so that numerous ingredients blend into a harmonious entity without losing their individual character. It is a cooking method eminently suited to an increasingly large number of fresh vegetables.

It is no wonder, then, that Americans have adopted stir-frying as a favored form of cooking, not only for Chinese dishes, but as a healthy way of preparing all kinds of vegetables, seafood and meat dishes.

The high heat is important; so much so that the Chinese term meaning "wok heat" is an expression for anything with great vitality. While it is possible to approximate the technique of stir-frying in a cast-iron frying pan, an aluminum paella pan or even a large sauté pan, the traditional Chinese wok is the only cooking pan that is ideally suited to stir-frying quickly, over high heat and with a minimum amount of oil. The wok is a wide conical-shaped pan with a curving base, somewhat like an inverted coolie hat. It usually comes with a special trivet or metal ring to support its base on a conventional stove top, but many cooks find that they can manage without it, preferring to get the pan closer to the heat source.

The procedure for stir-frying is very simple: The pan is heated, oil is swirled around, and seasoning ingredients such as chile peppers, gingerroot and garlic are added, releasing their aromas quickly into the hot oil. The main ingredients, usually vegetables, meat or fish, are added next, and seared quickly, tossing over high heat. Then, a small amount of liquid is usually added and the foods steam briefly, covered, until just crisp-tender. The pan is uncovered, final seasonings (and sometimes thickening) are added, and the food is tossed briefly to combine the flavors and evaporate the liquid to the point when the food is lightly coated with an even glaze.

Once you've grasped these simple fundamentals, an enormous range of dishes is within your grasp: stir-fried shrimps with vegetables, beef with hot black bean sauce, fried rice, Szechwan broccoli with garlic and minced pork, or chicken with hot chiles and cashews, lion's head (large pork meatballs), and many more.

The Japanese probably approximate the stir-fry most closely in their *teriyaki* dishes. *Teri* refers to the luster of the sauce that glazes the foods that are *yaki,* or broiled. One parallel, however, is that like the Chinese, the Japanese almost never use butter to panfry their foods. Dairy products are not native to this part of the world; their tastes and textures comprise a "basic palate" which is part of our Western learned experience, and this is simply not shared by people in the Orient.

Japanese flavor combinations are based on harmonious blends of soy sauce, *saké* (rice wine), and *dashi* (a basic stock made with dried bonito and kelp). In China, the ingredients typically used to season stir-fry dishes include soy sauce, sherry (used in the West as a reasonable substitute for *hwangjyou,* the rice-based "yellow wine" used for cooking in China), chiles (in certain regions such as Hunan and Szechwan), sesame oil, gingerroot and garlic.

Ginger, whose consumption has had portentous powers ascribed to it in many cultures, is known by many names. Probably a native of India or Malaysia, fresh gingerroot is widely used in stir-fry dishes for a warm, sweetly pungent flavor that is completely unlike ginger in its ground form. To store fresh ginger, peel the root and immerse it in a small jar of sherry or vodka; it will keep, refrigerated, for weeks, so you can slice off a small amount whenever you need it.

Garlic is another stir-fry ingredient which has inspired much cultural lore over the centuries. It has also lent its name to such sing-song culinary terms as *aïoli* (Provençal garlic mayonnaise) and *aglio e olio* (garlic and oil, for pasta). Until about 1930, garlic was widely held in low esteem; it was then used (in the West) mainly in the cooking of southern France and Italy, and in Spain. Currently, garlic-flavored dishes are enjoying great popularity, and have even inspired an annual garlic festival in California.

In Western cooking the technique that most closely approximates stir-frying is sautéing. *Sauter* is the French verb meaning "to jump." Vegetables, in order to be sautéed properly, should be cut into small pieces and cooked quickly, in a small amount of oil and/or butter in a large pan. While they are cooking they are made to jump around by shaking the pan back and forth over the heat. A large pan with sloping sides is best for sautéing; the vegetables should never be crowded so that they cannot move around freely while they cook. If the vegetables are crowded together or overlapping, they will produce steam and the final result will be limp and soggy rather than crisp and fresh.

Undoubtedly the most time-consuming part of both stir-frying and sautéing is the preparation beforehand, which can often be done well in advance of the actual cooking. The vegetables selected must be washed, peeled when necessary, and cut into small pieces. The traditional Chinese cutting tool is a broad cleaver, which is particularly useful to scoop up the diced vegetables after they have been cut. A sharp knife, however, will do just as well, and often a food processor will give the quickest, most efficient results. Vegetables that are cut by hand, using a cleaver or a knife, are traditionally cut on the bias for stir-frying. This allows a larger portion of the surface to be exposed to the heat and the vegetables cook more quickly.

There is no end to the variety of vegetables that lend themselves to stir-frying and sautéing. To a large extent the time of year still determines the quality and choice of vegetables but most supermarkets carry a pleasing selection all year round.

Not too long ago, vegetables occupied a position of lowly importance in any meal. In planning, service and preparation they were very much an afterthought. It is no wonder that children grew up hating the poor, spiritless veggies that came with dinner and traditionally preferred to eat their vegetables raw, snacking on crunchy carrots and crisp celery before they were ruined for dinner. Today's concerns about diet and health have made us realize the importance of vegetables in our diet. Experts in the fields of health and nutrition are recommending that we eat less meat and fat and more vegetables and complex carbohydrates. Vegetables, therefore, are no longer the stepchild of a meal. Although they are most frequently served as a side dish, there is no reason why a well-prepared dish of stir-fried vegetables cannot be served as the main course. With the addition of grains, such as brown rice or bulgur, or whole-grain pasta, they make a delicious, healthy meal that is low in calories and high in nutritional value.

Any combination of vegetables can be used in a stir-fry or sauté. Consider onions, scallions, carrots, cabbage (red and green and Savoy when you can get it), Chinese cabbage (bok choy), broccoli, cauliflower, zucchini, red peppers, green peppers, yellow peppers, radishes, mushrooms, celery, snap beans, snow peas, asparagus, tomatoes, cucumbers, spinach, kale, and every sort of sprout.

Whatever vegetables you choose, you should select them with a thought to freshness, texture, taste and color. As you prepare them to be stir-fried or sautéed, it is useful to separate them into two basic groups: the harder, longer-cooking ones, such as root vegetables, go into one and the softer, faster-cooking ones, such as zucchini, mushrooms, etc., go into the other. Your cooking should begin with the first group; the vegetables from the second should be added in the last few minutes. Ideally, stir-fried or sautéed vegetables should be served as soon as they are cooked.

SAUTÉING VEGETABLES

There are four types of pan-frying or shallow-frying used for vegetables: softening, sweating, browning and sautéing. The first three are usually preliminary steps to other cooking, but sautéed vegetables can be served without further cooking. All methods use some kind of fat. In softening, the vegetable pieces are cooked uncovered until partly or fully tender; the pieces are stirred or the pan is shaken to allow even cooking and to prevent sticking. In sweating, which might also be called oil-steaming, the pieces are cooked covered over very low heat until they release juices and almost melt, but because of the low heat they do not color at all. In browning, one starts with the softening process, then the heat is increased so that the pieces are colored or browned.

All vegetables can be sautéed. Large specimens need to be sliced or diced, but small ones can be sautéed whole. Hard vegetables such as turnips and rutabagas, carrots and stored parsnips, need to be parboiled (blanched) for best results; without this preliminary step, sautéing might leave the center of the vegetable still uncooked; or the longer time needed to cook through to the center might over-

Salting Vegetables

1 Wipe the vegetables clean with a damp cloth. Do not remove the skin.

2 Trim off the stalk end and the tip. Cut the vegetables into thin slices or small pieces.

3 Place a layer of slices in a colander. Sprinkle with salt and repeat after each layer.

4 Cover with a plate that fits snugly inside the colander to weigh down slices.

5 Set the colander where it can drain for about 30 minutes.

6 Rinse each slice thoroughly to remove salt and juices, and pat dry.

Sautéing Potatoes

1 pound waxy potatoes
½ to ¾ ounce butter
2 to 3 tablespoons oil

1 Parboil the potatoes, drain and dry them thoroughly. Cut into ¼ inch slices.

2 Put enough fat in a pan to make a thin layer, about ¼ inch deep. Place over low heat.

3 Increase heat to medium, add enough potatoes to just fill pan. Cook a few seconds.

4 Start to turn the potatoes with a spatula, and keep turning them regularly.

5 As the potatoes begin to absorb the fat, shake the pan over the heat to prevent sticking.

6 When the potatoes are cooked, lift them out with a spatula allowing excess fat to drain away.

7 Place the potatoes on 2-3 layers of paper towels to absorb any extra grease.

8 Slide potatoes from paper towels on to warmed serving dish. Sprinkle with herbs if wished.

cook the outside. Potatoes may be parboiled or not; if you choose to do it, start them in cold water and cook them for 3 or 4 minutes only. Any old and very large vegetable can be parboiled for more tender results. The time for parboiling depends on the size of the pieces and how hard the vegetable is; allow 2 to 8 minutes. Bring a large pot of water to a boil, add ½ teaspoon salt per quart of water, then drop in the vegetable pieces. Count the time from the moment when the water returns to the boil. Both fennel and celery will have a better texture if parboiled for 5 minutes before sautéing; without it, they develop a mushy texture in the sauté pan. Bell peppers will always be more delicious if peeled; if you do not peel them, parboil them for 1 minute. As soon as the vegetables are done to your taste, drain them, rinse with cold water, and drain again. If you plan to sauté them at once, roll them in kitchen paper towels to dry thoroughly. If you are doing this step in advance, let them drain dry and refrigerate as soon as cool.

Salting Vegetables

Some vegetables, such as eggplants and cucumbers that contain a lot of liquid, are often salted before sautéing. This is not necessary, but it does somewhat reduce the amount of oil that the vegetable absorbs. If you choose to do this, sprinkle slices or pieces with coarse salt or sea salt and arrange them in an enamel-lined or pottery colander. Cover with a plate to weight the vegetables and set the colander where it can drain for about 30 minutes. When ready to sauté, rinse thorougly to remove salt and juices, and pat dry. Do not salt the finished dish without first tasting it.

Sautéing Equipment

Almost any kind of frying pan that is large enough to hold the vegetables without crowding, and that is easily maneuvered over the heat, can be used for sautéing. There are special pans for this purpose. A *sautoir* has a thick base and low, outward-sloping sides; a *sauteuse* is also heavy and shallow like the *sautoir,* but its sides are straight. Both these sauté pans have long handles, and this is important so that your hand will not get splattered with hot fat as you are making the vegetables "jump around." However, any sturdy skillet or sauté pan, with a level base (not warped) and heavy enough to retain even heat, can be used.

Sautéing Technique

Choose the pan and set it over moderate heat. Add the cooking fat. Butter mixed with a little oil to prevent burning, or oil alone are the best choices, but bacon fat or lard may be used if the taste suits your menu. Oil alone is best for moist vegetables such as tomatoes, summer squashes and eggplants. Any good-quality vegetable oil may be used, and olive oil is also a favorite, but it has a pronounced flavor that does not suit all foods. Raw butter alone will burn and add unattractive dark flecks to the dish, as well as an unpleasant taste. Pour enough fat into the pan to make the thinnest possible layer, less than ⅛ inch deep. More can be added later if needed, but for sautéing the oil is merely a means to prevent the food sticking to the pan. Heat the oil but do not let it brown at all.

Add the vegetables in a single layer, ideally with no slices overlapping, or the moisture in the vegetables will cause steaming and prevent crisping. Have ready wooden spoons, spatulas or tongs to turn vegetables as they cook; do not use a fork as it will cause loss of juices. Also have ready a slotted spoon to lift out the finished vegetables. Let the pieces sauté for a few minutes, then turn them over. When the second side has cooked for a few minutes, reduce the cooking temperature to allow heat to penetrate to the center and finish cooking. If the vegetables are chopped or diced, turn them often as they cook. Try not to turn slices more than once or twice as too much turning will break them up.

When the vegetables are done—crisp outside and tender inside—lift them out with a slotted spoon, let as much fat as possible drain off, and transfer to a plate or baking sheet lined with absorbent toweling. If there are many pieces to be sautéed, use a baking sheet and keep the finished pieces warm in a low oven. Be sure there is enough fat in the sauté pan for the next batch. Reheat the pan to starting temperature, and continue until all are done. Any fat left at the end is discarded.

Do not salt or pepper the vegetables until sautéing is finished; however, minced herbs (sage, thyme, savory, parsley), finely chopped garlic, or grated citrus rinds can be added for the last minutes of cooking. Grated cheese or a mixture of cheese and crumbs can be sprinkled over just before serving. The cheese will melt slightly from the heat of the vegetables and add extra flavor.

STIR-FRYING VEGETABLES

The Chinese stir-frying technique is an ideal way to prepare vegetables. The finished vegetables are crisp-crunchy, with excellent flavor and usually heightened color. Cooking in water never gives these results. In stir-frying the cooking time varies with the ingredient—the way it is cut, its texture and natural tenderness. During cooking the pieces of food are stirred or tossed constantly, so that all sides are moved into the oil and the hottest part of the pan. The amount of oil used is always small; even less oil can serve if you invest in a wok.

Stir-Frying Equipment

A wok is one seamless piece of metal, usually iron, but today aluminum and stainless-steel woks are available also. The pan has handles on opposite sides. When you buy one to use on a conventional stove, it will come with a metal ring to enable the round-bottomed pot to stand level.

A cover is usually sold with a wok also, and it is useful for finishing some preparations. Seldom sold with the basic equipment are a few tools useful for stir-frying—a long-handled spoon with a curved shape and a curved slotted spoon or sieve. Round-bowled tools are easier to use in the round wok. Chopsticks are excellent for stirring, but they are not as easy for Westerners to use for turning pieces of vegetable as a curved spoon. If you don't have these tools, use long-handled wooden spoons.

The wok uses such a small amount of oil because of its shape. As the pieces cook and are pushed up the side, oil drains away and returns to the bottom, which is over direct heat. The food is never soaked in the oil; as a result, when finished it is not oily. If you stir constantly and do not fry for too long, vegetables will never be mushy or soft, but just tender.

While it is possible to stir-fry in a sauté pan or skillet, either pan will require more oil and the food will always be resting in the oil so that the final result is not quite the same.

Cleaning and Seasoning a Wok

Most traditional woks are made of iron, and professional chefs still consider these to be the best. An iron wok heats up very quickly and the heat is evenly distributed. Once it is removed from the heat, an iron wok cools down almost as rapidly as it heated up. With regular use and proper care an iron wok will eventually turn black and its inside surface will be as smooth and stick-free as any Teflon-coated pan.

If you have just acquired an iron wok, or the one you have has rusted or sticks, it is important to season it. The procedure is quite simple:

- Scrub the wok with a soapy scouring pad and rinse well with warm water. Dry it immediately.
- Place it over low heat and rub 2 tablespoons of vegetable oil into the surface with a soft, dry cloth. Do this for about 3 minutes.
- Use a vegetable brush and scrub the wok with ordinary kitchen soap under very hot running water.
- Dry it and oil it again over low heat, exactly as you did before.
- When the wok is cool enough to touch, rub your finger over the inside; if it feels greasy or sticky, repeat the steps until the pan is absolutely smooth to the touch.

Cleaning a Wok

An iron wok should be cleaned as soon as possible after each use. Remove every bit of food and wash it under hot running water while scrubbing it with a vegetable brush. *Do not use soap.* Dry it immediately over high heat for 15 or 20 seconds. If it should rust, then you must season it again.

Stir-Frying Technique

The favorite oil for stir-frying is peanut oil or sesame seed oil. Other vegetable oils can be used, but olive oil is not recommended as the odor is too pungent for the method. Use light oils; polyunsaturated seed oils are good. Whichever oil you choose, use it sparingly.

Before you start to stir-fry, everything must be fully prepared. The ingredients must be measured out; vegetables must be peeled and cut up or chopped; the seasoning and flavoring and any liquid to be used for finishing

Stir-Fry Preparation

1 *Shredding:* Pile leaves into stacks. Keeping tip of knife on board, raise and lower blade, cutting through stacks.

2 *Roll-cut:* Do not slice carrot, but make a diagonal cut straight down. Roll carrot a quarter turn, cut again. Continue process.

3 *Diagonal cut:* Hold knife or cleaver at 45-degree angle; cut vegetables into thin diagonal slices.

must be assembled. The preparation time may be considerable if you are cooking many vegetables, but the cooking time will be only seconds or minutes. Most Chinese dishes are served as soon as ready. Stir-fried foods can often be cooked between courses; at any rate they should be cooked at the last minute. If the finished stir-fried vegetables are left to sit in the wok, covered or uncovered, they will start to lose their crisp texture and bright color. If the wok is covered, steam will condense on the lid and drop into the pan, making the pieces mushy. When done, transfer vegetables to a dish for immediate serving.

The seasoning, flavoring and liquid used for finishing vary according to the vegetable and how it is to be served. Stock, soy sauce and rice wine are the most usual liquids. Stock may be chicken, beef or veal; in special cases broth made with pork or lamb bones or a stock made of vegetables may be used. There are several kinds of soy sauce—light, medium, dark; some are very salty. You will need to experiment to determine which kind you prefer. The usual commercial soy sauces are medium in color and saltiness. Rice wine is available in Oriental markets, but dry sherry is a good substitute.

The usual seasoning of salt and pepper may be omitted if you have used salty soy sauce or added a peppery flavoring such as fresh gingerroot. Garlic is a favorite Chinese flavoring. It can be peeled and added whole to the oil, to be retrieved and discarded later, or can be puréed and cooked with the vegetables. Onions, shallots and scallions can be chopped and added. Raw scallions are often added as a garnish to the finished dish. Gingerroot, peeled, is often cooked in the oil to flavor it; this, like whole garlic, is then discarded. Or the gingerroot can be minced and added to the vegetables to be mixed in and served with it. Condiment sauces; herbs, spices and seeds; vegetable purées, especially tomato; fruit juices, especially lemon; all these are used. The choice of these additions and the amount depends on the individual recipe. Aside from the garlic or gingerroot stir-fried at the beginning, these other ingredients are usually mixed together and poured in at the end of stir-frying. This liquid is brought to a boil, which will take only a minute as the wok is hot, and reduced to half, until the liquids barely coat the pieces of vegetable; they should not be drippy. The reduction should take no more than a minute. If honey or sugar is added, the vegetables will look glazed.

Vegetables for Stir-Frying and Sautéing

Cooking a single vegetable is simple but more often one is cooking a combination. In this case it is important to add the vegetables to the pan one at a time, starting with the one that needs longest cooking, or the one that is cut into largest pieces. A variation in size gives an interesting texture and appearance to the finished dish.

For 1 pound of vegetables, enough for 4 portions, cooked in a wok, you will need 2 tablespoons oil. More can be added if necessary, but always try to use the smallest possible amount. For cooking the same quantity of vegetables in a sauté pan, you will need 3 to 4 tablespoons oil. When the vegetables are finished and before the liquid and flavoring are added, you may want to pour off the oil remaining, or lift out the vegetables with the slotted spoon and blot up any oil. The wok is

Stir-Frying Vegetables

1 Have all ingredients ready. Pour oil, along with flavoring into wok. Heat over high heat until very hot.

2 Add vegetable. Using a quick, tossing motion, stir constantly with chopsticks or wooden spoon.

3 Pour in liquid and/or glaze, if being used. Mix well and stir-fry over high heat for 2 to 3 minutes longer. Serve at once.

wiped out with paper towels, then reheated. Vegetables are returned to the pan, the liquid mixture is added, and the dish is quickly finished.

Strong-flavored vegetables or less tender ones such as root vegetables are fine for stir-frying and sautéing if they are first blanched. The exact time for blanching depends on the vegetable. This is a sensible step, because those vegetables that need long cooking require less time after blanching, and there is no risk of their drying or burning through too long stir-frying. One other bonus—blanching can be done a day ahead to save time when preparing the meal. Vegetables should be well drained and patted dry before being put into the cooking oil.

Asparagus. Remove the tough parts of the stalk and discard or save for soup. If the asparagus is peeled, and it is always better so, it does not need to be blanched. Fresh, young asparagus needs only 5 minutes in the wok or sauté pan.

Beans. All varieties of snap beans are very good, including green beans, wax beans, Chinese long beans. The younger the better. Wash them, remove any strings, and snap them into halves, or slice them on the bias, or leave them whole, especially if they are young and small. Older or larger beans should be blanched briefly before sautéing or stir-frying for 5 minutes.

Broccoli. Separate the stems and florets. Peel the stems and cut into small pieces. May be blanched or not. Sauté or stir-fry for 5 to 8 minutes, according to the size of the pieces.

Cabbage. Use red, green or Savoy. Remove tough outer leaves and cut the head into quarters. Cut away the tough inside stalk and slice leaves into julienne. Blanching is not necessary as it cooks very quickly, but stored winter cabbages will have a more delicate taste after blanching. Cook for 3 minutes.

Carrots. Carrots are delicious in stir-fried mixtures as they add sweetness, crunchy texture and color. Wash, scrape, and trim. Cut into thin rounds or julienne, or use a roll-cut technique. Cook for 5 minutes, or until as tender as you like.

Cauliflower. Wash and break into small florets. Blanching is optional. Stir-fry or sauté for 5 to 7 minutes.

Celery. Adds crunchy texture, delicate taste and spicy aroma. Wash; cut away tough part of ribs and stringy portions. Cut into 1-inch chunks, roll-cut, or julienne. Cook for 3 to 5 minutes.

Chinese Cabbage. There are at least 3 species grown in China in northern, middle and southern areas, all available in American markets, although not always in supermarkets. Bok choy or Chinese chard is like a chard, with thick white ribs and dark green leaves. Pe-tsai or celery cabbage or nappa is more familiar, with its compact head like a pale thick celery stalk. All these cabbages are more delicate in flavor than ours. Blanching is not needed. Prepare like our cabbage, and cook for about 3 minutes.

Cucumber. Although it is often overlooked as a vegetable to stir-fry or sauté, it is delicious when prepared this way. Small, unwaxed cucumbers need not be peeled. If they are young, with few seeds in the center they need not be salted. Older cucumbers should be sliced and salted. Cook for 3 minutes.

Eggplant. Except for the very youngest, smallest eggplants (no longer than 3 or 4 inches) eggplants should be blanched or salted before stir-frying or sautéing. Cook for about 5 minutes.

Mushrooms. All edible mushrooms are delicious in a stir-fry or sauté, in combination with other vegetables, or on their glorious own. If you are lucky enough to get shiitake mushrooms, or chanterelles, or other wild mushrooms, do not hesitate to cook them this way. But even ordinary white cultivated mushrooms are very good. Wipe them clean and slice them. Cook 2 to 4 minutes.

Onions. Peel, cut into halves, and slice. Thicker slices will remain crunchy, thinner ones will wilt. Large white Bermuda onions with their mild flavor are perfect for these methods. Small white onions (silverskins) and pearl onions (white, yellow and red) can be stir-fried or sautéed whole if they have been first blanched briefly, which is convenient for making peeling easier. Cook 3 to 5 minutes.

Peas. Snow peas and sugar snap peas are both excellent, adding sweetness and great crunchy texture. Wash, remove strings, and snap into halves if they are large. Cook 2 to 4 minutes.

Peppers. Use green, red or yellow bell peppers, also the pale green Italian frying peppers. Peppers should be washed, stems, ribs and seeds discarded. Cut into strips, julienne or diamond shapes. Cook briefly to retain the crunchy texture, about 4 minutes.

Scallions. Trim, wash, and slice on the bias. Add at the very last minute and cook for only a few seconds.

Spinach. Tender, fresh spinach leaves are delicious stir-fried or sautéed. The leaves must be washed carefully to remove every bit of grit and dirt. Pick over the leaves and pull away any tough stems. The leaves will shrivel as they cook so slicing is not necessary. Cook 2 to 4 minutes.

Squash. Tender summer squashes—yellow crookneck and straightneck, pattypan or cymling, caserta and the related chayote—can all be sautéed or stir-fried. Peel unless the squash is young with very tender skin. Scoop out any mature seeds. Slice or dice, and stir-fry for 5 to 8 minutes.

Zucchini. The smaller they are, the better. Older, very large zucchini may benefit from being blanched or salted. Scrub with a vegetable brush. Peel only if zucchini are older, with tough skins. Cut into cubes or julienne. Cook 5 to 8 minutes.

Zucchini with Lemon-Parsley Butter

4 portions

- **8 zucchini, each about 4 ounces**
- **3 ounces butter**
- **2 tablespoons olive oil**
- **2 tablespoons lemon juice**
- **½ teaspoon salt**
- **½ teaspoon white pepper**
- **3 tablespoons chopped fresh parsley**

Wash and trim zucchini and cut them into ½-inch crosswise slices. Dry slices thoroughly on paper towels. In a large skillet over moderate heat, melt 2 ounces of the butter with the olive oil. When the foam subsides, add zucchini slices and sauté them for 8 to 10 minutes, stirring occasionally or shaking the pan to prevent sticking.

Add lemon juice, salt and pepper to the zucchini and stir in remaining butter and the parsley. When the butter has melted and zucchini is well coated with parsley, serve at once.

Zucchini Provençale

4 portions

- **8 zucchini, each about 4 ounces**
- **3 garlic cloves**
- **4 tablespoons olive oil**
- **½ teaspoon salt**
- **½ teaspoon white pepper**
- **2 ounces fine dry bread crumbs**
- **2 tablespoons chopped fresh parsley**

Wash and trim zucchini and cut them crosswise into ½-inch rounds. Dry slices thoroughly on paper towels. Peel and crush the garlic cloves. In a large skillet over moderate heat, heat the olive oil. When hot, add zucchini to the pan and sauté them for 8 to 10 minutes, stirring or shaking the pan to prevent sticking. Raise the heat to fairly high and stir in salt, pepper, garlic, bread crumbs and parsley. Remove pan from heat and toss the vegetables gently. Transfer mixture to a warmed serving dish and serve immediately.

Zucchini with Almonds

4 to 6 portions

- **2 medium-size onions**
- **1 pound zucchini**
- **4 ounces slivered blanched almonds**
- **4 tablespoons olive oil**
- **2 teaspoons lemon juice**
- **¼ cup dry white wine**
- **¼ teaspoon salt**
- **¼ teaspoon black pepper**

Peel and slice the onions. Wash and trim zucchini and cut into thin slices. Toast the almonds lightly. In a large skillet over moderate heat, heat the oil. When hot, add onions and sauté, stirring occasionally, for about 10 minutes, or until they are golden brown; do not let them burn on the edges. Add zucchini and sauté, stirring and turning frequently, for 8 to 10 minutes, until tender. Add lemon juice and wine and reduce the heat to low. Stir in almonds, salt and pepper, and sauté, stirring constantly, for 1 minute longer.

Remove pan from the heat and transfer the vegetables to a serving dish. This can be served hot, but it is just as delicious cold; to serve cold, let vegetables cool in the serving dish.

Summer Squash with Sage and Chives

6 portions

- **2 pounds yellow summer squash**
- **1 small onion**
- **3 tablespoons olive oil**
- **6 fresh sage leaves, or 1 teaspoon ground sage**
- **2 tablespoons snipped fresh chives**

Wash and trim squashes. Unless they are small and tender, peel them with a vegetable peeler. Cut them lengthwise into halves. If there are mature seeds, scoop them out with a melon-ball cutter. Cut the halves into ¼-inch crosswise slices. Peel and mince the onion.

Heat the oil in a large skillet over moderate heat. Add onion and sauté for 5 minutes, until onion is golden; do not let it brown. Add the squash slices and sauté, turning and tossing the pieces, for about 8 minutes, until squash is almost tender. If you are using fresh sage, snip the leaves with scissors and add to the squash. If you are using ground sage, sprinkle it in. Sauté, stirring, for 2 minutes longer; squash should be still crisp. Sprinkle with the chives and serve.

Cauliflower Sauté

4 portions

- **1 cauliflower, 1 to 1¼ pounds**
- **1 bay leaf or bouquet garni**
- **1 garlic clove**
- **1 lemon**
- **2 ounces butter**
- **2 ounces dry bread crumbs**

Cut the cauliflower into flowerets, or slice it. Blanch it in lightly salted water with a bay leaf or *bouquet garni* for 5 minutes. Drain well. Peel and crush the garlic. Squeeze the lemon. Melt the butter in a heavy sauté pan over low heat. Increase heat to medium, add garlic and cauliflower, and brown quickly, turning the pieces all the time. Remove cauliflower from the pan to a warmed serving dish and keep hot.

Brown the bread crumbs in the butter remaining in the pan, then pour in the lemon juice. Pour the lemony crumbs over the cauliflower and serve at once.

Broccoli with Black Olives

4 portions

- 1½ **pounds fresh broccoli**
- 1¼ **cups water**
- 2 **teaspoons salt**
- 3 **tablespoons olive oil**
- 1 **garlic clove**
- 6 **grindings of black pepper**
- ¾ **cup pitted black olives**
- 4 **tablespoons grated Parmesan cheese**

Wash the broccoli, remove leaves, peel the stalks, and break the flowerets into fairly large clusters. Bring the water to a boil in a large saucepan. Add 1 teaspoon salt and the broccoli and blanch the vegetable over brisk heat for 5 minutes. Reserve the blanching water and drain the broccoli. Rinse it with very cold water and drain again.

Heat the oil in a large skillet. Peel the garlic and put through a press into the oil. Sauté garlic for 2 minutes, then add broccoli and season with remaining salt and the pepper. Sauté broccoli for 10 minutes, stirring frequently. If the pan becomes too dry, add a few tablespoons of the reserved blanching water. Cut olives into halves and add to the pan. Sauté for 2 minutes longer, then turn broccoli and olives into a warmed serving dish. At once sprinkle with the Parmesan cheese; it will melt somewhat from the heat of the vegetables. Serve at once.

Sautéed Eggplant

4 portions

- 3 **eggplants, about 8 ounces each**
- 2 **tablespoons salt**
- 4 **tablespoons flour**
- 6 **tablespoons olive or vegetable oil**
- 2 **tablespoons chopped parsley**

Trim and peel the eggplants and cut them into ¾-inch cubes. Put cubes in a colander, sprinkle with the salt, and leave them to drain for 30 minutes. (Omit the salting if salt is not permitted in your diet.)

Rinse eggplant cubes, dry them on paper towels, and sprinkle them with the flour. Heat the oil in a large skillet over moderate heat. Add eggplant cubes and sauté them briskly, stirring now and then, for 10 minutes, or until cubes are tender. Remove eggplant cubes with a slotted spoon, put them in a warmed serving dish, and sprinkle with parsley.

Eggplant with Yogurt

4 portions

- **1 garlic clove**
- **½ cup plain yogurt or sour cream**
- **salt and pepper**
- **1 pound eggplant**
- **1½ ounces flour**
- **6 to 10 tablespoons olive oil**

Peel the garlic and put through a press into the yogurt or sour cream. Add plenty of salt and freshly ground black pepper. Mix well, and chill in the refrigerator.

Wash eggplant and trim the ends. Cut eggplant into ¼-inch slices. Place slices in a colander set over a draining board, and sprinkle the slices generously with salt. Cover with a plate that fits inside the colander and weight it. Let the eggplant drip for 1 hour, then rinse each slice thoroughly under cold running water and pat dry with kitchen paper towels. (Omit the salting if salt is not permitted in your diet.)

Season the flour with salt and pepper. Dip eggplant slices into flour to dust both sides. Shake off excess flour. Pour some of the olive oil into a sauté pan to reach a depth of ¼ inch, and place the pan over low heat. Raise the heat slightly and put a few slices of eggplant in the pan, not overlapping. Cook for 2 minutes, then turn slices over with a pancake turner and cook for 3 minutes on the second side. Remove cooked slices from the pan and keep hot in a dish lined with paper towels while you sauté the rest. Add more olive oil as needed until all eggplant is done. Drain the last batch and turn all the slices into a warmed serving dish. Serve the chilled yogurt sauce separately.

Mushrooms Sautéed in Butter

4 portions

- **8 ounces mushrooms**
- **1 garlic clove**
- **1½ ounces butter**
- **½ teaspoon salt**
- **¼ teaspoon black pepper**
- **1 tablespoon chopped parsley**

Wipe mushrooms with a damp cloth; do not peel them unless they are very soiled. Cut off the base of the stems. Cut caps and stems into thin slices. Peel the garlic. Melt the butter in a large skillet over high heat. When the foam subsides, put the garlic through a press into the pan. Sauté for 1 minute, stirring constantly. Add mushrooms and sauté them for 4 or 5 minutes, until lightly browned. Shake the pan so the mushrooms become coated with butter and brown evenly. Season mushrooms with salt and pepper. Remove pan from heat and sprinkle mushrooms with parsley.

This makes a small portion, an accompaniment to a main dish. To substitute for a vegetable, double the recipe.

Cucumber with Onion, Dill and Paprika

4 portions

- **2 cucumbers, about 8 ounces each**
- **1 large onion**
- **1 garlic clove**
- **3 tablespoons olive oil**
- **1 teaspoon dill seeds**
- **1 teaspoon paprika**
- **¼ cup chicken stock**

Peel the cucumber, removing the thinnest possible layer of peel, and cut cucumbers into thin rounds. Salt to drain off excess liquid, if desired. Peel the onion and cut into very thin slices. Peel and mince the garlic. Heat the oil in a large skillet over moderate heat. Add onion, garlic and dill seeds. Sauté until the onion is golden. Stir in the paprika, then add the cucumber slices. Increase heat to high and sauté for 1 minute, stirring the cucumber with 2 forks so it does not burn. Pour in the stock, bring it to a boil, and let the liquid reduce almost completely, leaving just a tiny amount of glaze on the vegetables. Serve immediately.

Sautéed Green Beans and Red Pepper

4 portions

1 pound fresh thin green snap beans
salt
2 large red peppers
1 white onion
3 tablespoons vegetable oil
1 teaspoon crumbled dried savory

Wash beans, top and tail them, and leave them whole. Put in a large saucepan, sprinkle with 1 teaspoon salt, and cover with water. Bring to a boil and blanch for 3 minutes. Drain in a colander and rinse with very cold water. Wash peppers, discard stems, ribs and seeds, and cut peppers from stem to blossom end into strips the same width as the beans, or narrower. Peel and mince the onion. (For a more delicate dish, the peppers can be charred first, then peeled.)

Heat vegetable oil in a large skillet over moderate heat. Add the onion and sauté for 2 minutes. Add pepper strips and sauté, stirring, for 5 minutes. Add the blanched green beans and the savory, and sauté the vegetables, tossing and turning to mix everything, for 5 minutes longer, or until the beans are as tender as you like them, but crisp is best.

This is a good dish for Christmas—green and red—and the vegetables are available in that season.

Sautéed Leeks with Mustard

4 portions

1 to 1½ pounds thin leeks
salt
3 tablespoons butter
1 tablespoon olive oil
1 teaspoon minced fresh savory or crumbled dried savory
4 tablespoons white wine
2 tablespoons prepared Dijon-style mustard

Wash leeks carefully; cut off roots and the top few inches of the green leaves. Cut the rest into round slices and put them in a large saucepan. Sprinkle with 1 teaspoon salt and cover with water. Bring to a boil, then simmer for 3 minutes. With a slotted spoon transfer leeks to a colander, rinse with cold water, and drain well. Discard blanching liquid.

Heat butter and olive oil in a large skillet over moderate heat and sauté the leeks, turning them often, until they turn golden and translucent. Sprinkle in savory and pour in the wine. Cook for a few minutes longer, until wine is almost evaporated. Stir in the mustard and mix gently.

These leeks are a good accompaniment to pork dishes and roast chicken.

Julienne of Celery, Potatoes and Green Pepper

4 portions

1 medium-size head of celery
1 medium-size green pepper
1 medium-size onion
3 large potatoes
2 ounces butter
1 tablespoon vegetable oil
1 teaspoon salt
¼ teaspoon crumbled dried thyme
1 teaspoon minced fresh chervil, or ½ teaspoon dried chervil

Trim and wash the celery; cut off the leafy tops (save to flavor soup) and cut the head across into 2-inch sections. Cut the sections lengthwise into julienne strips. Wash pepper, discard stem, ribs and seeds, and cut pepper lengthwise into julienne strips. Peel and chop the onion. Peel potatoes and cut into julienne strips. In a large skillet melt the butter with the oil. When foam subsides, add celery, green pepper and onion. Reduce heat to low and sauté, stirring occasionally, for 3 minutes. Add potatoes and sprinkle with salt, thyme and chervil. Sauté, stirring occasionally, for 8 to 10 minutes longer, until potatoes are cooked but still firm. Remove pan from the heat and serve at once, while everything is still hot.

Celery and Walnuts

6 portions

- **2 heads of Pascal celery**
- **3 ounces shelled walnuts**
- **1 tablespoon corn oil**
- **1 ounce butter**
- **salt and white pepper**
- **grated rind of 1 orange**

Wash celery, remove coarse outer ribs, and cut off the tops of the leaves. (Leaves can be saved to flavor stocks and soups.) With a chef's knife cut celery across to ½-inch slices. Chop the walnuts. Heat the oil and butter in a skillet and sauté the celery over moderate heat, turning it now and then, for 15 minutes. Add more butter if necessary. Add walnuts and sauté for another 2 minutes. Season to taste. Turn into a warmed serving bowl and sprinkle with orange rind.

Four-Onion Sauté

4 to 6 portions

- **2 small leeks**
- **1 pound small white onions (silverskins)**
- **12 to 16 green onions (scallions)**
- **3 tablespoons olive oil**
- **salt and white pepper**
- **2 tablespoons snipped fresh chives**

Trim leeks, wash carefully, and cut across to make ½-inch rounds, including the tender parts of the green tops. Cover leeks with water, bring to a boil, and boil for 2 minutes. Use a slotted spoon to lift leeks to a colander; rinse and drain them. Discard blanching water and rinse the saucepan (it may be sandy). Cut a cross in the root end of each white onion and drop them into the saucepan. Cover with water, bring to a boil, and boil for 5 minutes. Drain in a colander and rinse with cold water. Cut off the root ends and pop the onions out of their skins. Trim scallions and sliver both white and green parts.

Heat the oil in a large skillet and add the sliced leeks and whole white onions. Over moderate heat sauté the vegetables, turning them often to cook evenly, for about 8 minutes. Add scallions and sauté for 2 minutes longer, stirring all the while. Season with salt and white pepper to taste. Sprinkle in the chives and stir for 1 minute more. Transfer to a serving bowl.

An excellent accompaniment to beef dishes.

Glazed Onions

6 portions as a garnish

- **1 pound small white onions (silverskins)**
- **3 tablespoons butter**
- **2 tablespoons soft brown sugar**
- **1 tablespoon minced parsley**
- **½ teaspoon crumbled dried thyme**

Make a cross in the root end of each onion. Cover them with water, bring to a boil, and boil for 5 minutes. Drain and rinse. When cool enough to handle, peel the onions.

Heat the butter in a skillet and add whole onions. Sauté them, stirring often, for about 8 minutes, until they are golden. Test with a skewer; the onions should be tender. Sprinkle in the sugar and ¼ cup water and cook onions, stirring often, until the water, sugar and butter are reduced to a glaze. Sprinkle with parsley and thyme, toss to mix, and serve as a garnish to beef or lamb dishes.

To serve as a vegetable, double the recipe.

Variation: Sprinkle the glazed onions with grated Cheddar or Gruyère cheese to make a more nutritious dish, delicious served with rice or bulgur.

Parsnips with Cheese and Parsley

6 portions

- **1 pound parsnips**
- **salt**
- **1 tablespoon corn oil**
- **2 ounces butter**
- **¼ cup grated sharp Cheddar cheese**
- **¼ cup chopped fresh parsley**

Use a vegetable peeler to scrape parsnips. Trim them, and halve them lengthwise. Cut the halves on the diagonal into ½-inch pieces. Sprinkle with 1 teaspoon salt and cover with water. Bring to a boil and blanch parsnips for 3 minutes. Drain well and pat dry.

In a large skillet heat oil and butter together. Add parsnips and sauté over high heat, tossing and turning the pieces until they are buttered all over and tender. Pour parsnips and butter into a serving bowl and sprinkle cheese and parsley over them. Toss gently to mix, and serve at once.

Parsnips are enhanced by butter; the oil is used only to keep the butter from burning.

Sunchokes with Bacon and Cheese

4 portions

- **1 pound sunchokes (Jerusalem artichokes)**
- **6 slices of smoked bacon**
- **2 tablespoons lemon juice**
- **3 ounces Vermont Cheddar or other sharp cheese, grated**

Scrub the sunchokes, cover with water, and boil for 1 minute. Drain and rinse sunchokes. When cool, peel and slice them. Cut the bacon slices into ½-inch pieces. Put the bacon in a cold skillet and slowly heat it. Sauté bacon, stirring to cook all the pieces evenly, until fully cooked. Use a slotted spoon to transfer bacon pieces to a plate covered with paper towels. Pour off all but 2 tablespoons of the bacon fat. When bacon is cool, crumble it.

Reheat the skillet with the 2 tablespoons bacon fat. Turn in the sunchoke slices and sauté, stirring often, until they are golden. The pieces may break up, but that does not matter. Also, since these vegetables can be eaten raw, they can be cooked as briefly as you like. Pour in lemon juice and cook for another minute. Transfer vegetables to a warmed serving bowl and sprinkle first with the cheese, then with the crumbled bacon.

This makes a good main dish for a luncheon.

Rösti (Swiss Potato Cake)

4 portions

- **1½ pounds potatoes**
- **3 ounces smoked bacon**
- **1 onion**
- **4 tablespoons lard**
- **salt and pepper**

Cook the potatoes in their skins for 15 minutes. Drain and chill them. They are easiest to handle when they have been refrigerated overnight.

Peel skins from potatoes and grate potatoes on the coarse side of a grater. Cut the bacon into matchstick pieces. Peel and mince the onion. Melt the lard in a heavy sauté pan over low heat. Add bacon and onion and cook until softened. Increase heat a little and brown bacon and onion. Add the grated potatoes, season with salt and freshly ground black pepper, and sauté over medium heat. Occasionally loosen the mixture at the base of the pan and turn the potatoes over with a pancake turner. Cook for 30 minutes.

Press the potatoes down into the pan to form a firm cake. Cover with the lid of the pan, and continue sautéing until a golden crust has formed on the bottom, about 15 minutes.

To serve, invert the mixture onto a warmed dish, so the crusty golden surface is uppermost.

Broccoli, Chinese Style

4 portions

- **2 pounds fresh broccoli**
- **6 tablespoons peanut oil**
- **1 teaspoon salt**
- **½ teaspoon sugar**
- **1¼ cups chicken stock**
- **2 teaspoons cornstarch**
- **1 tablespoon cold water**

Wash the broccoli and separate stalks from flower heads. Cut the flower heads into fairly large clusters, and put the clusters in a bowl. Peel the stalks and slice them diagonally into 1-inch pieces. Discard the tough ends of the stalks. Put the stalk slices in another bowl.

Heat the oil in a large skillet or wok over moderate heat and add the sliced stalks. Stir-fry them for 1 minute. Add the flowerets and continue to stir-fry for another minute. Add salt, sugar and chicken stock. Stir well, cover the pan, and cook over moderate heat for about 8 minutes, until broccoli is tender but still crisp. Mix the cornstarch into the cold water and stir the mixture into the pan of broccoli. Stir for 1 minute, until the sauce thickens and becomes translucent. Transfer broccoli and sauce to a warmed serving dish and serve at once.

Stir-Fried Chinese Cabbage

4 portions

- **1½ pounds Chinese cabbage (bok choy)**
- **2 tablespoons peanut oil**
- **1 garlic clove**
- **½ teaspoon salt**
- **⅓ cup water**
- **2 teaspoons soy sauce**
- **1 teaspoon cornstarch**
- **½ teaspoon sugar**

Remove coarse outer leaves from cabbage, wash it, and shred it by hand or on a mandoline. Heat the oil in a wok over moderate heat. When oil is hot, add the garlic and cook, moving it around constantly, for 1 minute. With a slotted spoon remove and discard the garlic. Add cabbage and salt to the pan and cook, stirring, for 6 minutes. In a small bowl or cup, beat water, soy sauce and cornstarch with a fork until the mixture is smooth. Stir in the sugar. Pour the mixture into the wok, stirring as you pour, and cook cabbage for 2 minutes longer, stirring constantly. Remove pan from heat and transfer cabbage to a warmed serving dish. Serve at once.

Stir-Fried Carrots, Celery and Turnips

4 portions

- **1 head of celery**
- **4 small white turnips**
- **2 carrots**
- **1 large potato**
- **2½ tablespoons unsalted butter**
- **1 tablespoon vegetable oil**
- **¼ cup chicken stock**
- **¼ teaspoon crumbled dried thyme**
- **salt and pepper**
- **1 tablespoon minced fresh parsley**

Trim celery, cut it into 2-inch lengths, and cut these sections into julienne strips. Peel turnips, carrots and potato, and cut all of them into julienne strips. In a wok or large skillet, heat the butter and oil over moderate heat. When foam subsides, add celery, turnips, carrots and potato. Stir-fry the vegetables for 5 minutes. Pour in chicken stock and stir for 1 minute. Add thyme and salt and pepper to taste. Stir-fry for 3 minutes longer. Vegetables should be still crunchy.

Transfer vegetables to a warmed serving dish. Sprinkle with parsley and serve.

Stir-Fried Vegetable Hash

2 to 4 portions

- 1 garlic clove
- 1 inch piece of fresh gingerroot
- 2 carrots
- 1 small green pepper
- 1 very small head of cauliflower
- 2 ounces bean sprouts
- 3 tablespoons vegetable oil
- ½ teaspoon salt
- ¼ teaspoon pepper
- ⅔ cup chicken stock
- 2 teaspoons soy sauce
- 1 teaspoon soft brown sugar

Peel and crush the garlic. Peel gingerroot and slice it very thin. Scrape carrots and slice thin. Wash pepper, discard stem, ribs and seeds, and shred pepper. Trim and wash cauliflower and break it into small flowerets. Wash bean sprouts and shake them dry.

Heat the oil in a wok over moderate heat. When hot, add garlic, gingerroot, salt and pepper. Stir-fry for 1 minute. Add carrots and stir-fry again for 1 minute. Add green pepper and cauliflower and stir-fry for 3 minutes. Add bean sprouts and stir-fry for another minute. Stir in stock, soy sauce and sugar. Cover the wok and cook for 3 to 4 minutes, until liquids are reduced to hardly more than a glaze.

Remove wok from heat and immediately turn the vegetables into a warmed serving dish. Serve at once, while they are still crunchy.

Stir-Fried Cauliflower with Parsley

4 portions

- 1 pound head of cauliflower
- 1 medium-size onion
- 1 garlic clove
- 3 tablespoons olive oil
- ½ cup chicken stock
- 2 tablespoons dry white wine
- 4 tablespoons chopped fresh parsley

Break the cauliflower into florets of even size. Peel the onion and cut into thin slices; halve the slices. Peel and mince the garlic. Heat the oil in a skillet over moderate heat. Add the vegetables and stir-fry for 2 minutes. Pour in stock and wine and add the parsley. Bring liquids to a boil, cover the pan, and cook over moderate heat for 7 minutes. Serve immediately.

There should be only a few tablespoons of liquid remaining.

Five-Vegetable Stir-Fry

4 to 6 portions

- 1 large celery knob
- 1 large white Bermuda onion
- 2 green peppers
- 12 ounces mushrooms
- 10 ounces plum tomatoes
- 1 garlic clove
- 3 to 6 tablespoons olive or peanut oil
- salt and pepper

Peel celery knob, slice it, and cut the slices into thin strips. Put in a bowl and cover with water until you are ready to cook. Peel and slice onion and cut slices into quarters. Wash peppers, discard stems, ribs and seeds, and cut peppers into 1-inch pieces. Wipe mushrooms with a damp cloth, trim the stems, and cut caps and stems into thick slices. Blanch and peel the tomatoes and chop them. (For a more delicate dish, the seeds can be removed.) Peel the garlic.

Heat 3 tablespoons of the oil in a large skillet. Add the whole garlic clove and sauté for 2 minutes. Lift out and discard the garlic. Add drained celery knob strips and sauté for 2 minutes, tossing and turning the pieces all the time. Add onion and sauté for 2 minutes longer. Add pepper and sauté for 3 minutes. At each stage keep turning, tossing, and mixing the vegetables. Add more oil as needed. Add mushrooms and sauté until mushrooms release their liquid. Finally add the chopped tomatoes, sprinkle everything with salt and pepper to taste, and sauté and stir for a few minutes longer, until the tomatoes are softened and everything is well mixed and tender. Celery knob and pepper should still be crisp. Transfer to a serving platter and serve promptly.

This combination is excellent with fish dishes.

Bean Sprouts with Ginger

4 portions

- 1 large onion
- 1 inch piece of fresh gingerroot
- 3 tablespoons peanut oil
- 1 teaspoon salt
- 1 pound fresh bean sprouts

Peel the onion and cut into thin slices. Peel the gingerroot, cut into slices, and cut the slices into thin strips. Heat the oil in a wok over high heat. Add the onion slices, reduce the heat slightly, and stir-fry onion for 6 minutes. Use a wooden spoon for stirring. Add gingerroot strips and stir-fry for 4 minutes longer. Add salt, stir to mix, then add bean sprouts. Raise the heat and stir-fry bean sprouts, tossing and turning them rather than stirring them, for only 2 or 3 minutes. Serve at once.

This is delicious with any meat or poultry dish.

Bean Sprouts with Green Peppers

6 portions

- **2 pounds fresh bean sprouts**
- **2 large green peppers**
- **4 tablespoons peanut oil**
- **3 tablespoons white wine**
- **2 teaspoons salt**

Soak the bean sprouts in cold water for 15 minutes. Drain well. Wash green peppers, quarter them, and discard stems, ribs and seeds. Cut the quarters into thin, almost threadlike strips. Heat the oil in a wok or skillet over high heat. Add bean sprouts and pepper strips and stir-fry for 3 minutes. Add wine and salt. Still stirring, sauté for 2 more minutes. Serve hot.

Spicy Szechwan Eggplant

4 portions

- **1¼ pounds eggplant**
- **1-inch piece of fresh gingerroot**
- **¼ cup sesame-seed oil**
- **6 whole Szechwan chiles, or 1 teaspoon crushed hot red pepper**
- **1 tablespoon soy sauce**
- **2 tablespoons bottled oyster sauce**

Peel eggplant and cut into julienne strips. Peel and slice gingerroot. Heat sesame oil in a wok over high heat. Add gingerroot and chiles and stir-fry for 1 minute. Add eggplant and stir-fry for 2 minutes. Stir in soy sauce and oyster sauce; stir-fry for 1 minute longer. Spoon eggplant onto a warmed serving dish and serve at once.

Sesame-seed oil, Szechwan chiles and oyster sauce can be found in Oriental markets and in many large supermarkets that stock Oriental foods. This dish is very hot; if you like a milder dish, omit the chiles or crushed hot pepper.

Kachang Bendi Goreng (Stir-Fried Green Vegetables and Shrimps)

4 portions

- **2 onions**
- **1 garlic clove**
- **2 green chiles**
- **1 inch piece of fresh gingerroot**
- **1 green pepper**
- **½ pound fresh thin green snap beans**
- **2 zucchini, about 6 ounces each**
- **¾ pound fresh raw shrimps**
- **3 tablespoons peanut oil**
- **1 tablespoon ground almonds**
- **2 tablespoons soy sauce**
- **½ teaspoon black pepper**

Peel and chop onions; peel and crush garlic. Using rubber or plastic gloves, cut chiles open, rinse out seeds, and cut out ribs. Mince the chiles. Peel gingerroot and mince it. Wash pepper, discard stem, ribs and seeds, and cut pepper into thin slices. Wash and trim the green beans, but leave them whole. Wash and trim zucchini; do not peel unless the skin is very tough. Cut zucchini into crosswise slices. Peel and devein shrimps.

Heat the oil in a wok. Add onions, garlic, chiles and gingerroot; stir-fry over medium heat until onions are golden brown. Add almonds, soy sauce and black pepper; stir-fry for 1 minute. Add the shrimps and stir-fry for 2 or 3 minutes. Stir in remaining vegetables. Reduce heat to medium-low and stir-fry the mixture until vegetables are crisp-tender.

Transfer the mixture to a warmed serving dish. Serve immediately.

Snow Peas with Chinese Mushrooms

4 portions

4 dried Chinese mushrooms
6 ounces canned bamboo shoots
¾ pound fresh snow peas
1 celery rib
1 tablespoon vegetable oil
1 teaspoon salt
½ teaspoon sugar
1 teaspoon white-wine vinegar

Soak dried mushrooms in cool water for 30 minutes. Drain mushrooms, but reserve and filter the soaking liquid. Cut mushroom caps into thin slices; discard the stems as they are tough. Drain bamboo shoots; if they are not already sliced, slice them. Wash snow peas and pull off strings on both sides. Trim celery and cut diagonally into 1-inch pieces.

In a wok or large skillet, heat the oil over medium-high heat. When oil is hot, add sliced mushrooms and bamboo shoots; stir-fry for 2 minutes. Add snow peas and celery and stir-fry again for 2 minutes. Sprinkle salt, sugar, vinegar and 1 tablespoon of the mushroom soaking liquid over the vegetables. Stir-fry for 2 minutes longer, until liquid has evaporated.

Transfer vegetables to a warm dish and serve. Or, to serve as a cold salad, let them cool, cover with plastic wrap and chill for at least 1 hour.

Green Beans with Apples and Almonds

4 portions

1 pound fresh green snap beans
1 medium-size onion
2 large cooking apples
3 cups water
1 teaspoon salt
3 ounces unsalted butter
¼ cup slivered blanched almonds

Wash beans, drain well, top and tail them, and snap each bean across into halves. Peel the onion, cut into thin slices, and separate the slices into rings. Peel and core apples, and chop them. In a large saucepan bring the water with the salt to a boil. Add beans and cook, uncovered, for 5 minutes. Drain beans and set aside.

Melt the butter in a large skillet over moderate heat. Add onion rings and chopped apples. Sauté, stirring often, for 5 minutes. Stir in beans and almonds. Reduce heat to low. Continue to sauté, stirring frequently, for 5 to 7 minutes, until beans are tender. Transfer the mixture to a warmed vegetable dish, and serve while everything is still crisp.

Part Four

PIES AND TARTS

From Tom Sawyer through the Little Rascals, and right up to today, a freshly baked pie cooling on a windowsill has been a sign of irresistible temptation. Foods wrapped in crisp, flaky pastry have always had a special appeal—just think of berry pies, elegant French tarts, or the family of turnovers and pastries, and you'll realize why a cook's pastry is a sign of his or her skill.

Although pastry plays an important part in many ethnic cuisines, pies are a particularly American treat—indeed, "America's favorite dessert." The very term "as American as apple pie" reflects this; though, ironically, early Americans brought this popular dish from England. The word pie is of obscure origin, although the Oxford English Dictionary tells us that it was evidentally a popular word as far back as 1362.

What is the essential appeal of foods wrapped in pastry, and of the pie in particular?

Bernard Clayton, Jr., in his excellent guide, *The Complete Book of Pastry,* best sums up the reasons why the pastry makes the pie: "If the crust is tender, flaky, crisp and above all (or below all) not soggy, the crust can add a dimension that ranks pie with the best pastry creations in kitchens both here and abroad. A favorite filling may be the excuse to eat pie, but it should be the crust that makes the occasion memorable."

For all its appeal, pastry probably intimidates home cooks more than any other single item. Once you get the *feel* of making pastry (which is the only way to do anything, after all), it's easy as . . . well, pie. Use a light touch, work relaxed but quickly, and you'll find that making pastry can be one of the most enjoyable parts of cooking.

Cooks have been rolling pastry for centuries. In Ancient Rome, simple flour and water pastes were wrapped around meats to seal in juices. These were not eaten, but were used as festival decorations.

The word pastry is a form of the word paste, and this is still the term—*pâte*—used in French. In fact, pastry was called paste in English until fairly recently. This term lingers today with *pâte feuilleté,* often called puff paste.

Gradually, cooks added fat to the crude flour and water mixtures, and the pastry began to be eaten on its own merits. Frequently, pastry was used to protect delicate items such as custards from harsh oven heat (a form of edible *bain marie*), resulting in a flan or quiche.

In Renaissance Italy, a pastry case called a *timballo* (*timbale* in French) was used to serve pasta and entrée items. In France, pastry chefs moved on from the private employment of aristocrats and began to serve their confections in their own shops, called *pâtisseries.* One of the things Americans most enjoy on European visits are these pastry shops (called *Konditorei* in German), where one can sit and enjoy a small tart and coffee while inhaling the wonderful aroma of buttery pastries fresh from the oven.

The English have a special fondness for good meat pies, and their delicious Melton Mowbray pie has justifiably brought them international fame. At one point in their pie-baking history, some Englishmen used to think of a crust as a sturdy case for the pie, to protect the contents when sending the pie as a gift or taking it on a picnic, and hardly worth eating. Cottage pie, a hearty English dish prepared with Sunday's leftover meat and potatoes, was often so badly made, the British food authority Jane Grigson reports, that it "ruined our Mondays."

In the American colonies, pies were favorites early on. Bernard Clayton quotes an immigrant who wrote to his Norwegian friends that, using fresh berries, "they make a wonderful dish combined with syrup and sugar which is called pai. I can tell you that pai is something that glides easily down your throat. . . ."

The early brick ovens did not make easy work of baking pies and pastries, which were generally not placed in the oven until the heat had cooled somewhat after bread was baked. There is some disagreement about which colonies did the most to popularize pie as our favorite native dessert. In New England, colonists maintained English traditions with savory pies of chicken and veal, and clams and native lobsters were baked in pies along with balls of lobsters forcemeat.

In the South, meat pies were also popular, but local sweet tooths were soon appeased with pecan pies and chess pies. Thomas Jefferson, an avid gourmet, loved macaroni pies. Southern Blacks, of course, did much to develop a rich culinary tradition in the South with pumpkin, sweet potato, and squirrel pies.

Pies were not only a delicious way to enjoy the local produce; they also provided energy to hard-working farmers throughout America. Well into the nineteenth century, pies of every sort were standard breakfast fare throughout rural America. Records of the quantities of pies baked and consumed are often quite startling. Evan Jones mentions a Vermont housewife who counted 421 pies baked in 1877 (not to mention many more loaves of bread, doughnuts and cakes), and an old New England custom was to bake 50 to 100 mince pies each November, which were then stacked in covered stone crocks and stored in the woodshed.

In Pennsylvania Dutch country, there's a saying that "a meal without pie may be no meal at all." Local favorites there include shoo-fly pie, *rosina,* a lemon and raisin pie served at funerals, and "preaching pies," used to distract restless children during church services. In fact, the Pennsylvania Dutch, famous for their fondness for sweets, are also credited with having no fewer than 50 kinds of dessert pies in their culinary repertoire.

Nineteenth-century American cooks commonly referred to apples as "pie timber," and indeed apple pies were made so routinely that according to James Beard many old American cookbooks did not bother to include recipes because it was taken for granted that every housewife had her own favorite version.

In *American Food,* Evan Jones quotes a memoir of nineteenth-century Michigan by Della Lutes who describes her mother's apple pie, as a masterpiece that any cook might envy: "The crust was flaky, crisp, and tender. She used lard, and she mixed this with flour until it 'felt right.' She poured in water with a teacup, or the dipper, or whatever was at hand, but she never poured too much or too little. She laid on to the lower crust a bed of sliced apples to exactly the right height for proper thickness when the pie was done. It was never so thick that it felt like biting into a feather bed, nor so thin that your teeth clicked. It never ran over, and it had just the proper amount of juice. She sprinkled sugar over it with neither mete nor measure, and allspice and cinnamon from a can. But when the pie was done (crimped around the edges and golden brown on the humps, with an 'A' slashed in the top crust) it was a masterpiece of culinary art. With the edge of the oven's heat taken off, but never allowed to chill, and a goodly piece of cheese from the neighboring factory alongside, here was a dish which the average citizen of any country rarely meets."

And truly, in America, pies are a national glory. Parisians flock to an American hangout just to sample "*Les pies américains.*" And still very much in fashion is the pride of the home cooks who bring their specialties to country fairs throughout America each summer in hopes of winning a blue ribbon.

Happily, the days of freshly baked pies are not behind us, and even an imperfect home-baked pie in every way surpasses the soggy, stale, boxed supermarket variety. Making your own pastry is not at all difficult, whether you use your fingers, a knife and fork, or a pastry cutter. In recent times, the greatest aid to making pastry at home has been the introduction of a food processor. The food processor makes excellent pie pastry in minutes and many cooks claim that they would own a food processor for this alone.

The freezer, too, is of great value for planning ahead. For once you have made a batch of pie pastry, one-pie portions of pastry dough can be wrapped and stored in the freezer for several months. You need only remember to remove the dough in time to defrost overnight in the refrigerator to be ready to make fresh pies for any occasion.

Once you've mastered the basic short-crust pastry, it's simple to vary the dough, for extra richness or crisp strength. Soon, you'll be setting perfect pies on your windowsill to cool, and you'll find that you've acquired a well-deserved reputation as a pastry cook of the first order.

PASTRY

Pastry doughs are made of 3 ingredients—flour, fat and liquid. Variations in all three and the way they are combined give an enormous range of recipes suitable for pies, tarts, turnovers, pasties, rolls, etc. To make pastry that holds together well so the filling does not escape and at the same time have tender flaky pastry, the ingredients must be handled with care. You must develop enough gluten to make the dough manageable but not enough to make it tough, so the techniques are different from those used in making bread doughs.

Measure ingredients carefully for pastry doughs. Too much fat makes the pastry crumble, too much flour makes it dry and hard. The amount of liquid is small, but enough must be used so that the pastry does not break or crumble.

Pastry doughs should have a minimum of handling and should be kept cool. Do not mix with your hands until the very end because the heat of your hands will cause the fat to melt rather than to break into tiny flakes or crumbs. When you finally get to the stage when hands are essential, cool them in cold water and dry thoroughly; even then use only fingertips. The water added must be cold also. Use very cold tap water or ice water. The amount of water is small but not constant as each batch of flour will vary in its capacity to absorb. Add the water a teaspoon at a time, then a few drops at a time.

For pastry use plain flour, not cake flour or self-raising. You may use all-purpose, unbleached, whole-wheat, or mixtures of these, or a flour designed for these recipes called "pastry flour." All flours for pastry should be sifted before being measured by volume. After being measured either by weight or volume, sift them again and at the same time sift the salt used for the recipe so that it is well mixed in. Lard, vegetable shortening or butter are the usual fats; a mixture of half lard or shortening with half butter gives good texture and flavor. Butter alone gives excellent flavor but a firmer texture. Soft fats such as margarine or melted fats and oil give a sandy texture to the pastry. If the fat is cold and hard, the pastry will be flakier; if it is soft, pastry will be sticky.

Basic Short-crust Pastry

If you could have only one pastry, this would be the choice. It is the most flexible for all uses—good for tarts, flans, quiches; pies with single or double crusts; turnovers and pasties; patties, barquettes, canapé bases; casings for various fillings and wrappings for meat.

Make short-crust pastry following the techniques shown. When you have gathered the dough into a cohesive ball, place it on a cool unfloured surface and push it, bit by bit, away from you, flattening with the heel of the hand. Assemble the pieces again and repeat the process. This develops just enough gluten. It is not kneading but ruffling or flattening the pastry (*fraiser* in French). Pat the dough into a flattened ball, wrap in plastic wrap, and refrigerate for 30 minutes, or up to overnight. This relaxes the gluten so that pastry is not tough.

Plan for your specific use before rolling out the dough; if possible roll it out once, for re-rolling tends to toughen it (more gluten is developed) and you may absorb more flour from the rolling surface, giving a less tender pastry. If you plan to make 2 tart crusts or a dozen small pastry cases, cut the ball of dough into 2 or 12 pieces, and roll out each one to fit.

Remove the ball of dough from refrigerator and let it rest at room temperature for 15 minutes so it softens slightly; if you work with dough cold from the refrigerator it may crack. While dough softens, preheat the oven to the necessary temperature. The hot oven causes rapid expansion of the air trapped in the dough and gives light texture to the pastry. Dust your working surface with a little flour; use a sieve or shaker to have only a light coating. If you have too much, brush it aside.

Pâte Brisée (Short Pastry with Whole Egg)

This is a tart pastry without sweetening, and it can be used for all the uses of the short pastry. Traditionally the dough is mixed on a marble slab, which remains cool.

Sift flour and salt onto the working surface. Make a well in the center. Cut the butter into small pieces and drop into the well along with the lightly beaten whole egg. Using the fingertips of one hand, mix the ingredients in the well together. Pull the flour into the well, bit by bit. Add the water, tablespoon by tablespoon, working the mixture into a dough. Ruffle the pastry as usual, flatten it into a round, then wrap in wax paper and refrigerate for 30 minutes before using.

This pastry uses 2 cups of flour, 6 tablespoons of butter, pinch of salt, 1 whole egg and 4 tablespoons water. It is sometimes more buttery and it does break easily, hence its name. To make it less fragile, refrigerate overnight before rolling it out. In spite of its more fragile quality, this can be used in any recipe that calls for short pastry, or you can substitute short-crust pastry for this.

Pâte Sucrée (Sweet Tart Pastry with Whole Egg)

This is another delicious pastry for tarts. The chief difference in the ingredients is the addition of 2 tablespoons superfine sugar and 4 more tablespoons butter. Like *pâte brisée,* this is traditionally mixed on a marble slab. If you need water, add it a few drops at a time. Sometimes vanilla extract is added, up to 1 teaspoon. With this dough you can fill the unbaked pastry and bake shell and filling together, as

Short-Crust Pastry

Makes ½ pound

2 cups all-purpose flour
½ teaspoon salt
2 ounces unsalted butter or margarine
2 ounces lard or vegetable shortening
8 teaspoons ice water, approximately

The pastry dough will be easier to work if you use ice water. Cool your fingertips on the ice cubes before handling the pastry.

1 Sift flour and salt into a bowl. Add fats cut into chunks. Use a knife to cut fats into flour to pea-size pieces.

2 With cool fingertips, rub mixture together until mixture resembles bread crumbs. Let the crumbs fall into the bowl.

3 Shake bowl to bring lumps to the surface and rub in these lumps until fat is evenly distributed.

4 Sprinkle in 2 teaspoons of the water and mix it in with the round-bladed knife.

5 Sprinkle in another 2 teaspoons water and mix until dough begins to form small lumps.

6 Add another 2 teaspoons water and use the flat of the knife to press mixture into fairly large lumps.

7 Add remaining water. Clump the dough together, and draw all loose particles into the ball.

8 Place dough on an unfloured surface and ruffle it briefly. Wrap dough in plastic wrap and chill in refrigerator.

the pastry is strong enough to hold its shape. Or, bake blind partly or completely, according to your filling.

Pâte sucrée is traditionally used to make open-faced pies and tarts. These are particularly elegant when filled with pastry cream and topped with fresh uncooked berries—strawberries, raspberries, blueberries—alone or in colorful combinations.

Tarts, Flans and Quiches

For any of these you will need an ovenproof pie plate of metal, ceramic or ovenproof glass, with a wide enough edge to seal the pastry and prevent shrinking during baking. Or a flan ring, either a plain ring or a ring with fluted sides and removable bottom. Or a flat porcelain dish with fluted sides, designed especially for quiches.

Place the ball of dough on the floured surface and pat it out into a round. With a rolling pin, lightly dusted with flour or covered with stockinette, roll out pastry to a circle ⅛ inch thick and about 1 inch larger than the diameter of the pie plate. Place the plate upside down on the dough to measure it if in doubt. The extra width of pastry allows for the depth of the dish.

Once the pastry is in place, the edge should come just about even with the edge of the pan or dish. Roll a rolling pin over the edge to cut off excess pastry. Pinch the edge between thumb and forefinger and press it firmly against the fluted edge of the pan. It will stick up above the edge slightly, but will be even with it when baked. There is no thickened or doubled edge on these pans.

Always fill a tart with decorated edge after—not before—you have finished decorating.

Baking Blind

This process is done when the filling for the tart needs no baking or only

Short-Crust Pastry (Food Processor Method)

Makes ½ pound

1½ cups all-purpose flour
4 ounces cold unsalted butter, cut into 1-inch pieces
½ teaspoon salt
¼ cup ice water

• Once the dough has formed into a ball, wrap it in wax paper and refrigerate for 1 hour; or place it in the freezer for 20 minutes. It will be much easier to roll out.

• For a sweet pastry crust add 2 tablespoons of granulated sugar in step 1. The resulting dough will be delicately sweet, crisper, and a bit more fragile to handle.

• For additional flavor add a few drops of vanilla extract to the ice water.

1 **With metal blade in place add flour, butter and salt to work bowl of food processor.**

2 **Process for 8 to 10 seconds, until mixture has the consistency of coarse meal.**

3 **With processor running, pour ice water through feed tube in a steady stream.**

4 **When dough forms ball, stop processing. Turn onto wax paper, shape into 2 flattened discs; use at once or refrigerate.**

Pâte Sucrée (Sweet Tart Pastry with Whole Egg)

makes 12 ounces

- 2 cups all-purpose flour
- ¼ teaspoon salt
- 6 ounces unsalted butter
- 2 tablespoons superfine granulated sugar
- 1 large egg
- ¼ teaspoon vanilla extract (optional)
- 1 tablespoon cold water

Small amounts of water may be needed. Without the water, some sweetened pastries will crack, causing the filling to leak out. Add the water a few drops at a time, in steps 3 and 4, until the texture of the pastry is just right.

- Keep the pastry, the rolling surface and your hands as cold as possible, for sweet pastries become warm quickly.

- Additional flour can make pastry tough. Therefore roll it out between 2 layers of wax paper or plastic wrap. When the sheet of dough reaches the desired thickness, the wax paper or plastic wrap can be peeled off easily.

- This pastry, like most others, will have a better texture and will be easier to roll out if it is prepared 24 hours before you plan to use it and stored in the refrigerator. The reason is that the gluten developed in mixing has a chance to relax.

- *Pâte sucrée* can be stored in the freezer for 3 months. Defrost it in the refrigerator for 24 hours before you plan to use it.

1 Sift flour and salt onto a marble slab or pastry board. Make a well in the center of the flour.

2 Cut butter into small pieces and put into the well. Add the sugar, lightly beaten egg, and vanilla if desired.

3 Using fingertips, draw butter, sugar and egg together, until egg and sugar are well mixed. Add water if needed.

4 Work flour into the moist mixture, a little at a time. Scrape fingers with spatula if dough sticks to them.

5 When all flour is incorporated, ruffle the dough to homogenize it. Finally flatten dough again into a ball.

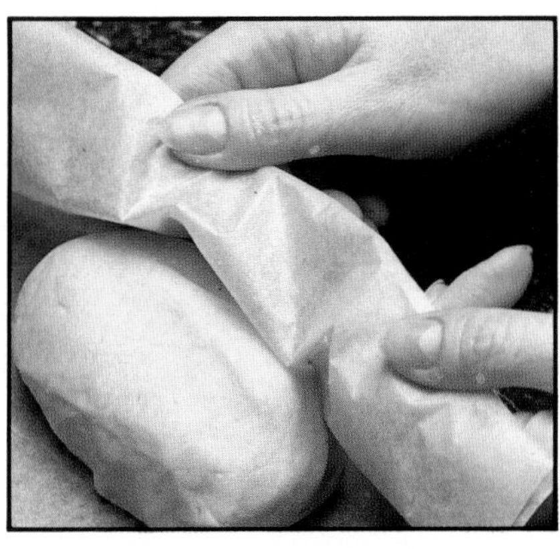

6 Wrap the dough in plastic wrap or wax paper and refrigerate for 1 hour, until pastry is firm.

brief baking; in such a case the pastry would not be baked enough or the filling would be baked too much without baking the crust first. Also, it is done for any kind of tart when the filling is very moist, like custard, and would tend to sink into the bottom of the dough before it had a chance to bake; that would make the pastry soggy.

Savory Tarts or Flans

These can be baked in any of the pans suggested, and can be served hot, cold, or at room temperature depending on the filling.

The fillings are most often completely cooked and bound together in a thick well-flavored sauce. The sauce may be béchamel or velouté, but always thicker than usual. Cold mixtures may be bound with mayonnaise or sour cream, flavored to suit the filling.

Sweet Tarts or Flans

Pumpkin pie is a typical American example of a sweet tart. It is always baked without a top crust, although sometimes it is decorated with a lattice. This filling is basically a thick custard, and a similar filling can be made with sweet potato.

Fruits are delicious in baked tart shells. Strawberries and blueberries, finished off with a glaze of cornstarch and sugar or of melted and strained apricot jam or currant jelly, look as good as they taste.

If you are concerned about the filling softening the bottom of the pastry, here are 2 solutions: Melt and strain

Lining a Pie Plate

1 Roll out pastry $\frac{1}{8}$ inch thick, 1 inch larger than the pie plate all around.

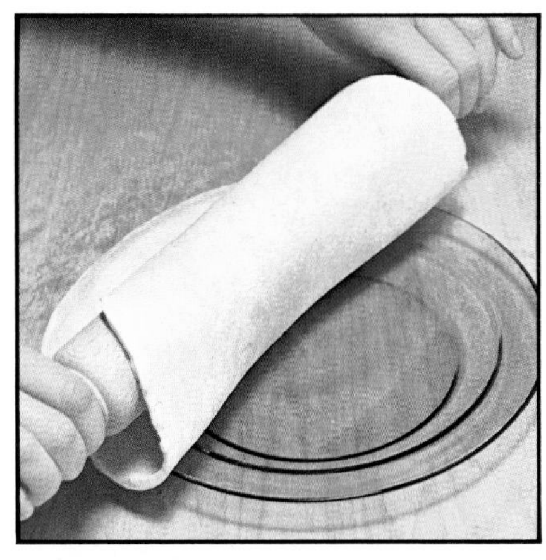

2 Roll the sheet of pastry on the pin and unroll it on the plate, centering it.

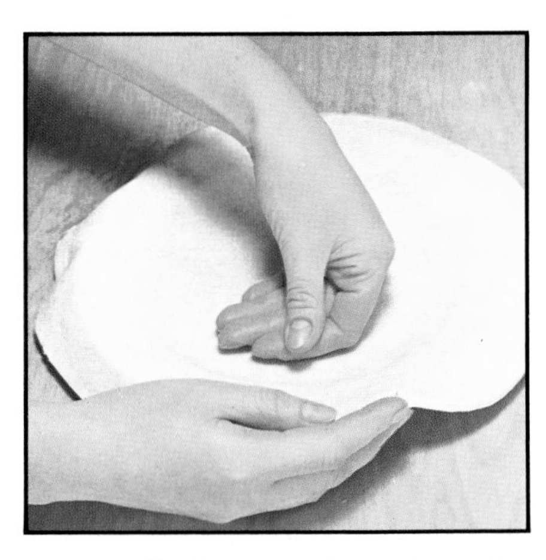

3 Working from the center to the edges, press pastry gently into place.

4 Prick base all over with a fork, to release any air trapped under the dough.

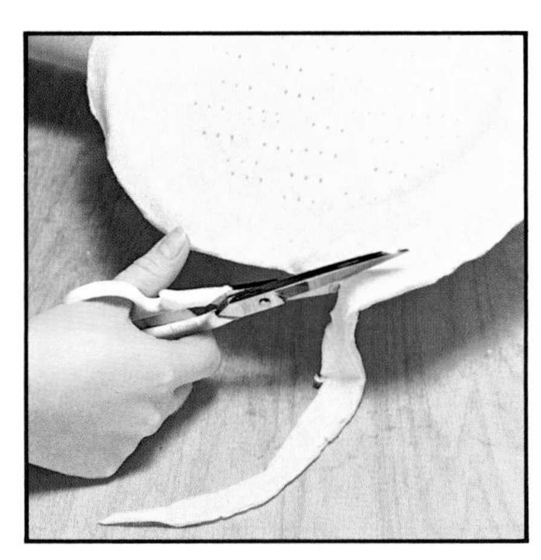

5 Use kitchen scissors to trim dough to an even $\frac{1}{2}$ inch all around the edge.

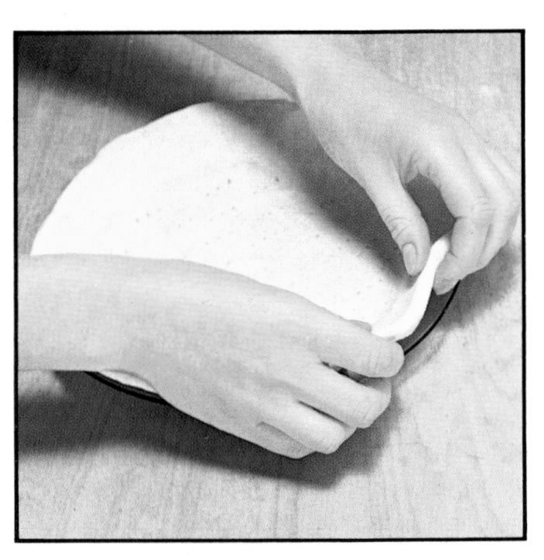

6 Fold the extra dough under the edge to make a thick rim all around, even with the dish.

apricot jam or currant jelly, plain or flavored with liqueur; let it cool slightly, then brush it over the inside of the partly baked shell. Let it set before filling. Or beat an egg white until foamy, brush it all over the inside of the pastry, and let it set before filling.

Turnovers

These are usually half-moons—a large or small round folded in half—but of course can be triangles, rectangles or ovals. The filling is placed on one half of the dough, the dough is flipped over, the moistened edges are sealed and crimped. Make steam vents and glaze.

Tartlets

These are just small versions of the larger tarts. The dough is cut into portions and each portion is rolled out to fit the tartlet pan; or the dough is rolled out to a large rectangle or round and a plain or fluted cutter is used to cut as many rounds as possible from the sheet. Either way, the rounds should be ½ inch larger than the diameter of the tartlet tins. After tartlets are baked, let them cool completely. Then gently slide a round-bladed knife between pan and pastry and lever the tarts out.

Pies

In America a pie is a pastry dish with a bottom crust that may have a top crust or not. In England a pie is a pastry dish with a top crust that may have a bottom crust or not. A fruit pie with a pastry top is sometimes called a cobbler, but in

Lining a Flan Ring

1 Roll out pastry to a round 1½ inches wider all around than the diameter of the ring.

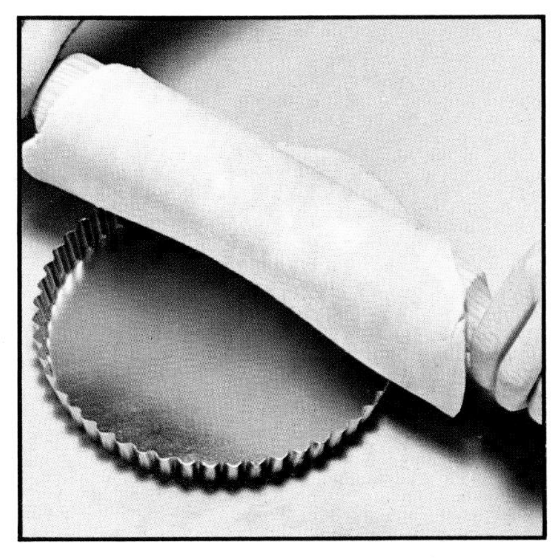

2 Roll dough on the pin and center it over the ring. Let dough fall into place.

3 Working from the center out, press dough snugly into the ring, fitting it closely to bottom and sides.

4 Roll the pin over the edge of the ring to cut off the excess pastry.

5 Press pastry between two fingers to fit it snugly into the flutes all around the ring.

6 Prick the bottom of the dough to release any trapped air. Chill the dough-lined flan ring until ready to fill it or bake it.

America a cobbler is a fruit dish with a biscuit topping. And so it goes.

Single-Crust Pies. These pies are usually baked in deep dishes. A pie funnel (or pie bird) is handy for pies with soft or juicy fillings. The funnel sticks up through the center of the pastry, to allow steam to escape. An upturned custard cup or egg cup, useful for the top pastry to rest on, is better for pies made with short pastry; the funnel piercing the crust may cause cracking of the crust.

Double-Crust Pies. These are made in the same dishes or plates as the single-crust pies, but often the dish is shallower. Make the amount of pastry needed for your pie or pies, chill it, then remove from refrigerator to soften slightly. Divide the batch of dough into 2 pieces, one slightly larger than the other. The larger piece is for the bottom crust. Roll out the bottom piece in the usual way, roll it up on the pin, and drop it into the dish. Work it into the dish from the center out, as with any short pastry. Spoon in the filling, mounding it up in the center. Roll out the second piece of dough, roll it up on the pin, and gently unroll it over the filling, centering it. Lift up the edge of the pastry and moisten the edge of the bottom piece. (It is better not to do this until the top is centered and in place, because you don't want it to stick until you are ready.) Press the 2 edges together, cut off excess, and flute the edge or crimp it with the tines of a fork. Decorate if you like, as for the single-crust pie. Make steam vents with a sharp knife or a skewer and glaze the top.

Baking Blind

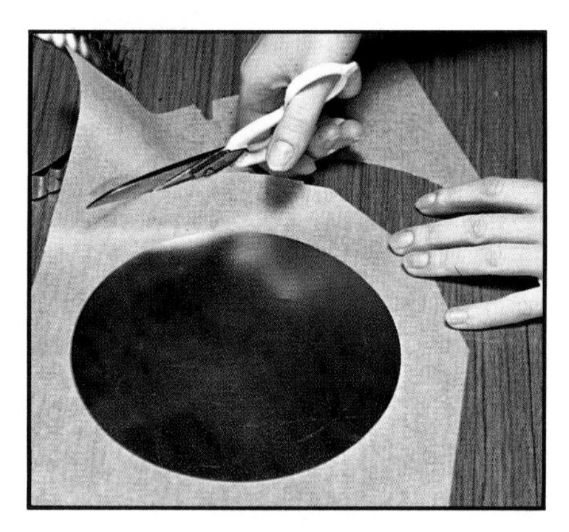

1 Cut a circle of foil or wax paper (foil preferred) about 3 inches larger than the diameter of flan ring or tart pan.

2 Crumple wax paper until soft, smooth out, then place it or foil into the pastry-lined pan.

3 Fill foil with dried beans or ceramic or aluminum pie pellets, making a thick layer around sides. Place pan on baking sheet.

4 Bake at 400°F on the shelf above the center of oven for 10 minutes. Remove from oven and lift out liner and weights.

5 For partial baking, return pan to oven and bake for 3 to 5 minutes longer, until pastry is just set.

OR For complete baking, return pan to oven and bake for 5 to 10 minutes longer, until pastry is dry and slightly brown.

Turnovers

- It is important to work quickly so that the pastry does not dry out.

- Keep a bowl of ice water nearby to moisten and cool your fingertips.

- Filled and folded turnovers may be wrapped in plastic and frozen for future use. No need to defrost. Simply add 5 to 10 minutes to the baking time.

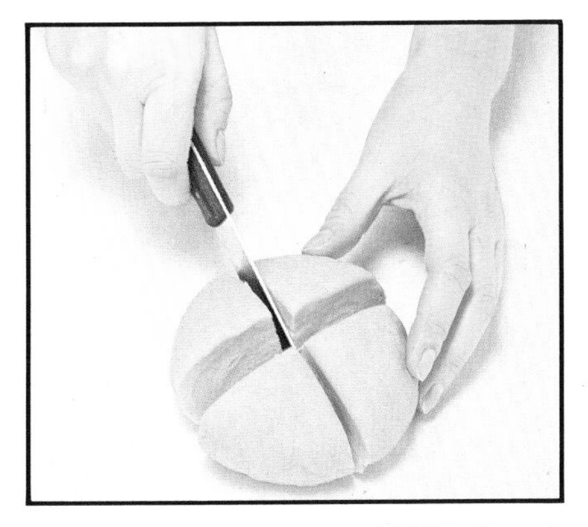

1 Preheat oven to 400°F. Cut ½ pound pastry into 4 equal portions. Pat each into a round.

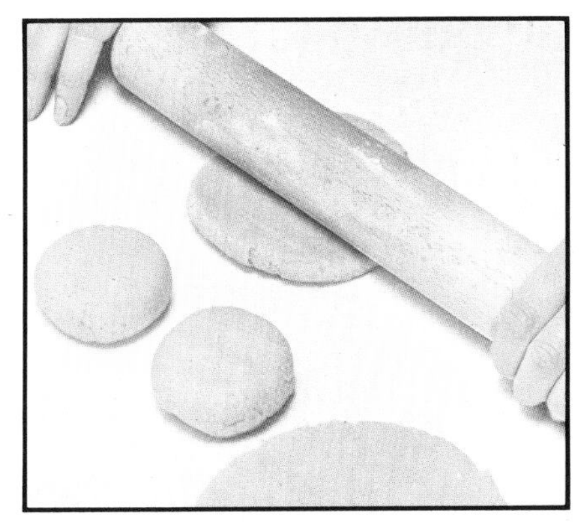

2 Roll out each round on a lightly floured board to a 6-inch circle.

3 Spread filling on half of each circle. Be careful not to spread any filling on the outer ½-inch edge of the circle.

4 Moisten edges of pastry with cold water. Fold one half over, line up the edges, and press firmly to seal.

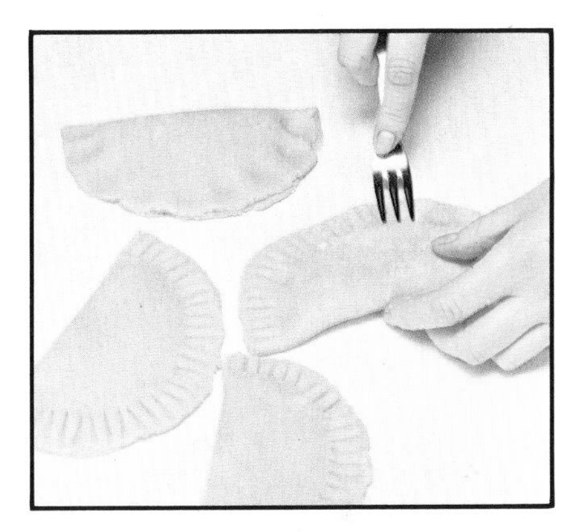

5 Press edges with tines of a fork to decorate and to reinforce the seal.

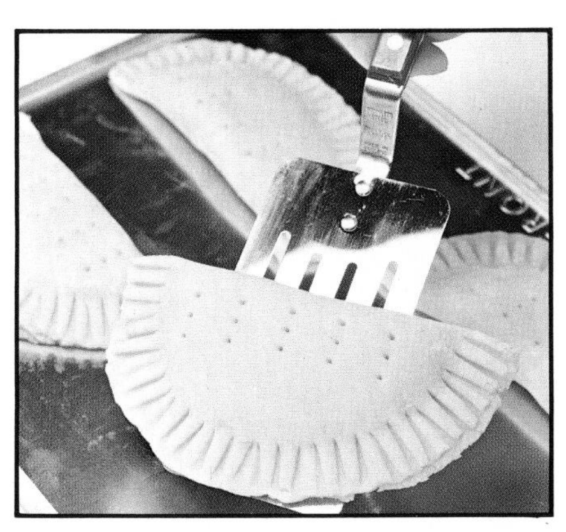

6 Prick holes in the top of each turnover for steam to escape. Lift turnovers to an ungreased baking sheet.

7 Brush tops of dessert turnovers with a little milk or beaten egg white and sprinkle with granulated sugar to give a crisp finish.

8 Bake on the shelf above the center of the oven for about 20 minutes. Dust with a little more sugar or some spice to serve.

Decorating Edges of Pies

1 *Forked:* Press tines of a fork into the folded pastry edge all around to make a pattern.

2 *Daisy:* Press handle of a teaspoon or butter knife against pastry rim all around to make a pattern.

3 *Goffered:* Slip a knife blade under the pastry edge, lift it slightly, and tuck the edge evenly all around.

4 *Sunflower:* Do not fold edge under; cut into 1-inch strips. Fold each diagonally, making series of triangles around edge.

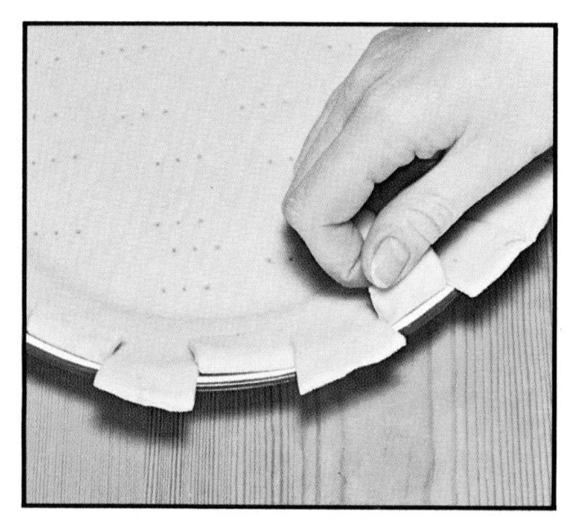

5 *Castellated:* Do not fold the edge under, but cut into 1-inch strips. Fold alternate strips in half and tuck under the edge.

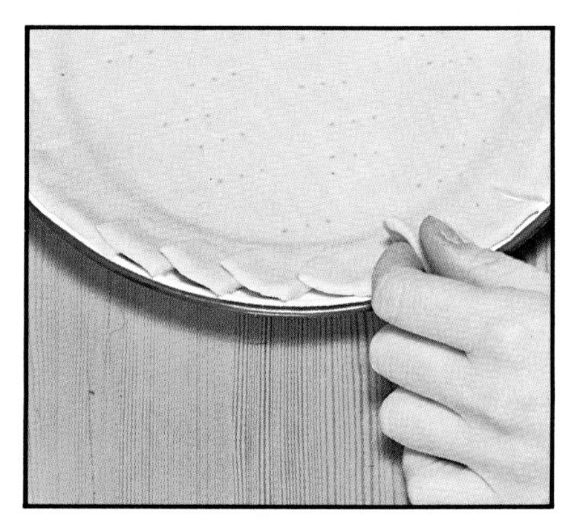

6 *Overlapping:* Fold the edge under and cut all around into ¾-inch strips. Bend each strip to overlap the next one slightly.

7 *Necklace:* Roll pastry trimmings into tiny balls. Moisten edge with water. Place balls on the damp edge and press lightly to seal.

8 *Diamonds:* Roll pastry trimmings into 1-inch strips; cut diagonally into diamonds. Moisten edge, overlap diamonds, press to seal.

9 *Braid:* Roll pastry trimmings into strips, braid them, and place evenly around the moistened edge of the dough. Press to seal.

Lattices

1 *Simple Lattice:* Roll pastry trimmings to a rectangle ⅛ inch thick and ½ inch longer than the tart plate.

2 Cut rectangle into strips ½ inch wide, with a knife or scalloped pastry wheel.

3 Moisten pastry edge of filled tart. Place half of strips across tart in parallel rows.

4 Place remaining strips across the first, at right angles. Trim ends of strips and press to seal to the moistened edge.

1 *Interwoven Lattice:* Place pie plate upside down on a sheet of wax paper and draw outline in pencil. Cut out the circle of paper.

2 Roll out pastry trimmings and cut into strips for lattice. Space half on the wax paper circle.

3 Working from one side and then the other, interweave remaining strips, leaving spaces between the strips.

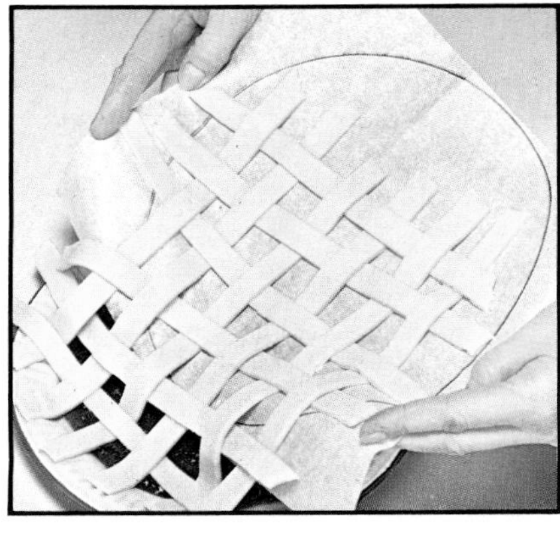

4 Moisten pastry edge of filled tart. Gently shake the lattice from the paper and ease it into place on top of the tart.

5 Trim ends of pastry strips even with the dish. Seal ends by pressing against the moistened pastry edge.

Blackstock Pie

8 portions

- 8 ounces Short-Crust Pastry (see Index)
- 4 or 5 Granny Smith or other tart apples
- 6 ounces Cheshire Cheese
- 1 egg white
- 2 tablespoons light brown sugar
- 1 tablespoon granulated sugar
- ¾ cup heavy cream

Cheese is a time-honored accompaniment to apple pie. In this traditional English pie, the cheese is baked in the pie and cream is added later.

• Use firm, tart apples; if you do not have Granny Smith, use Greenings.

• Toss apple slices in fresh lemon juice to prevent discoloration.

• Sharp Cheddar can be substituted for Cheshire cheese.

• Brush the uncooked pastry with egg white to help keep it crisp.

• Steam vents help release moisture which would otherwise make the pastry soggy.

• This pie is baked at two temperatures: the first, which is higher, helps the crust to brown and set firmly; the lower temperature that follows helps the crust and filling to bake through gently.

• Bake the pie in its dish on a heavy sheet pan, to cook the bottom crust thoroughly.

• Pour cream through the steam vents with care; a small funnel will help prevent spills.

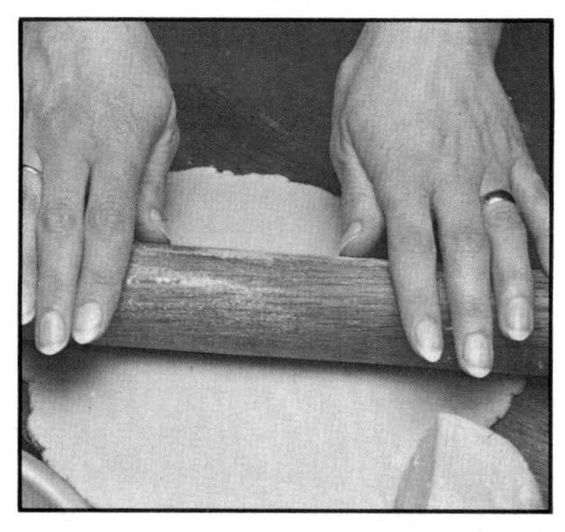

1 Roll out slightly more than half of the pastry and use it to line a 9-inch pie dish.

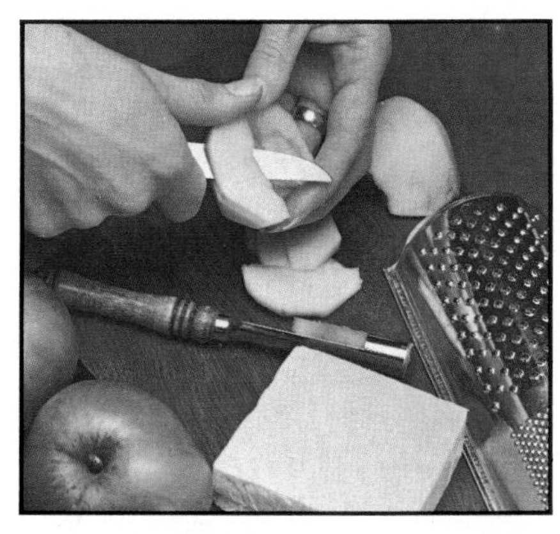

2 Peel and core the apples and cut into thin slices. Grate the cheese. Preheat oven to 400°F.

3 Brush the inside of the pastry and the rim of the dish with some of the egg white.

4 Pack half of the apple slices in the pastry. Sprinkle with half of the brown sugar and half of the cheese.

5 Repeat step 4, using remaining apples, sugar and cheese so the dish is filled.

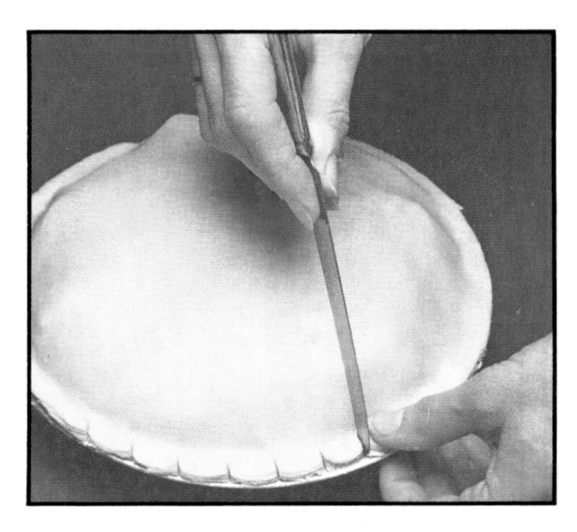

6 Roll out remaining pastry and lay it on top of the apples. Trim, seal both edges together, and flute or crimp the edges.

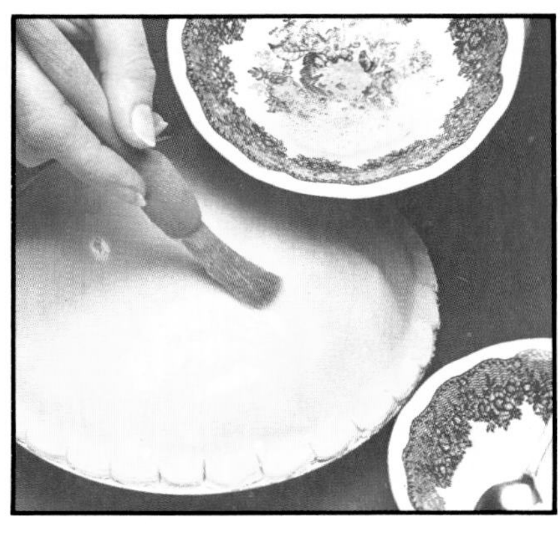

7 Brush the top of the pastry with remaining egg white. Sprinkle with the granulated sugar.

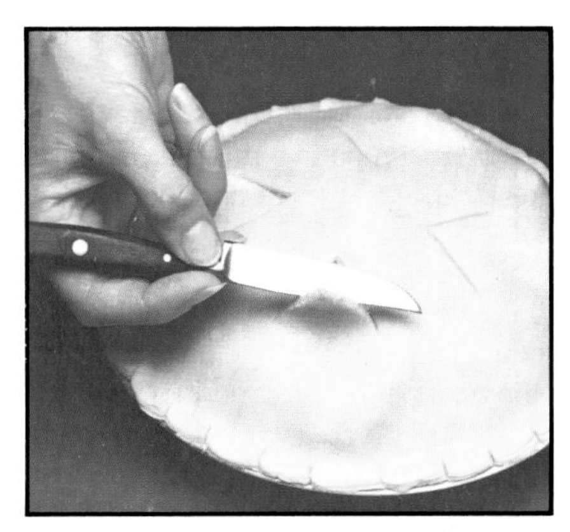

8 Cut 4 arrow-shaped slits in the pastry. Open up the pointed end of each slit, but do not detach it.

9 Bake for 25 to 30 minutes, until lightly browned. Reduce heat to 350°F and cook for 20 to 25 minutes longer.

10 Cool the pie slightly. While cooling, heat half of the cream to the scalding point.

11 Pour the hot cream carefully through the slits into the pie. Whip remaining cream to serve with the pie.

Macadamia Nut Tart

6 portions

- 8 ounces Short-Crust Pastry (see Index)
- ¾ cup shelled macadamia nuts
- 2 eggs, separated
- ¼ cup granulated sugar
- 1¼ cups milk
- 1 teaspoon unflavored gelatin
- 2 tablespoons cold water
- ⅛ teaspoon salt
- ¼ cup dark rum
- 1 cup heavy cream

Preheat oven to 400°F. Roll out the pastry and use it to line a 9-inch flan ring. Bake the pastry and cool it completely. Lift off the ring and place the baked shell on a serving plate.

Toast the macadamia nuts lightly and chop into pieces about the size of dried beans. Combine egg yolks and sugar in the top pan of a double boiler over barely simmering water in the lower pan. Heat the milk to scalding and pour it into the egg mixture. Cook the custard for 5 to 6 minutes, until thick, stirring all the time. Soak the gelatin in the cold water. Stir softened gelatin and chopped nuts into the custard and mix thoroughly. Set custard aside to cool. When cool, chill until thick but not set.

Beat the egg whites until soft peaks form. Add salt and continue to beat until stiff peaks form. Gently fold egg whites into the custard, along with the rum. Spoon the filling into the flan shell. Chill for 1½ to 2 hours, or until the filling is set.

Shortly before serving time, beat the cream until stiff. Spread whipped cream over the filling. Serve the tart immediately; if there is delay, chill it, but only briefly.

Cherryberry Pie

6 portions

- 1 pound rhubarb
- 5 ounces granulated sugar
- 4 ounces raspberries
- 4 ounces red currants
- 8 ounces cherries
- 6 ounces Short-Crust Pastry (see Index)
- milk
- granulated or confectioners' sugar

Preheat oven to 400°F. Wash and trim the rhubarb and cut the stalks into 1-inch lengths. Arrange rhubarb in the bottom of a 4½-cup pie dish. Sprinkle rhubarb with half of the sugar. Rinse and dry the other fruits; strip tiny stems from the currants and pit the cherries. Add raspberries and red currants to the rhubarb, then add remaining sugar, and finally add the cherries.

Set aside some of the pastry for decorations. Roll out the rest to a round 1½ inches larger than the top of the dish. Cut off a strip and press it on the moistened rim. Arrange the pastry lid on top and press to the rim to seal. Trim and flute the edge. Raise the pastry slightly in 2 places on opposite sides to let steam escape during baking. Roll out reserved pastry and cut into small circles, leaves and tiny strips to represent stems. Brush the top of the pastry with milk and gently stick the decorations to the surface to resemble a bunch of cherries. Brush the top of the decorations with milk.

Bake the pie for 15 minutes, then reduce oven temperature to 350°F and bake for 35 minutes longer. Dust the top of the pie with a little granulated or confectioners' sugar.

Somerset Spiced Apple Pie

4 to 6 portions

- 1⅛ cups medium-dry cider
- 1 cinnamon stick
- 3 whole cloves
- large pinch of freshly grated nutmeg
- 1½ pounds cooking apples
- ½ orange
- 3 ounces brown sugar
- 4 ounces Short-Crust Pastry (see Index)
- milk
- granulated sugar

Pour the cider into a large saucepan. Break up the cinnamon stick and add to the cider together with the cloves and nutmeg. Bring cider slowly to a boil, then boil vigorously for 3 minutes, or until reduced to about one third of the original quantity. Pour cider into a bowl and set aside until cold.

Preheat oven to 400°F. Peel, core, and slice the apples. Grate the orange rind. Pack half of the apples in a 4-cup pie dish and sprinkle on the brown sugar and orange rind. Pack remaining apples on top, mounding them in the center. Strain the cider to remove whole spices and pour into the apples.

Roll out the pastry ¼ inch thick and 1½ inches larger than the top of the pie dish. Cut off a strip and press it on the moistened rim of the dish. Place the round of pastry on top and press to seal to the moistened rim. Flute the edges. Raise the pastry slightly in 2 places on opposite sides to allow steam to escape during baking. Use pastry trimmings for decorations (an apple with 2 leaves). Brush the pastry liberally with milk, then sprinkle with granulated sugar.

Bake the pie for 20 minutes, then reduce oven temperature to 350°F and bake for 40 minutes longer.

Chestnut and Raisin Pies

12 individual pies

- **1 ounce fresh white bread**
- **2 ounces raisins**
- **8 ounces canned sweetened chestnut purée**
- **1 tablespoon rum or rum flavoring (optional)**
- **8 ounces Short-Crust Pastry (see Index)**
- **milk**
- **confectioners' sugar**

Grate the bread to crumbs and chop the raisins. A food processor works best for both steps. Spoon the chestnut purée into a bowl. Add bread crumbs, raisins, and rum or rum flavoring if used. Stir to mix.

Preheat oven to 400°F. Grease 12 tartlet pans, even if they are nonstick pans. Roll out the pastry ⅛ inch thick. Using a cutter the same size as the opening of the tartlet pans, cut out 12 lids for the pies. Using a cutter 1 inch larger than the first, cut out as many bases as you can from remaining pastry. Layer the trimmings together, roll out again, and stamp out the needed number of other rounds. Line the tartlet pans with the larger rounds, pressing them in to fit. Divide the filling evenly among the pans. Brush the edges of the lids with cold water and place them, damp side down, over the filling. Press the edges of the lids to seal to the bottom pastry. Pierce to make a steam vent and brush the tops with milk.

Bake the pies on the upper center shelf of the oven for 20 minutes, until the pastry is crisp and golden. Remove pies from the oven but leave them in the pans for a few minutes. Remove pies from the pans, using a palette knife if necessary. If you are serving the pies cold, put them on a wire rack to cool. Dust with confectioners' sugar when completely cold. If you are serving the pies hot, dust with confectioners' sugar and serve at once.

Congress Tarts

12 small tarts

- **4 ounces Short-Crust Pastry (see Index)**
- **1 tablespoon strawberry or raspberry jam**
- **2 ounces unsalted butter**
- **¼ cup sugar**
- **½ cup ground blanched almonds**
- **1 teaspoon grated lemon rind**
- **1 egg white**

Preheat oven to 400°F. Roll out the pastry and line 12 small tart pans. Spread about ¼ teaspoon jam in the bottom of each tart. Set pans aside in a cool place.

Prepare almond filling: Beat butter and sugar until light and fluffy. Blend almonds and lemon rind into the mixture. Whisk egg white until stiff and glossy; fold into the almond butter. Spoon filling evenly into the prepared pans and smooth the tops.

Bake the tarts for 20 minutes, until filling is set. Cool tarts in the pans before removing them to serve.

Latticed Apple Pie

6 portions

- **2 pounds cooking apples**
- **1 lemon**
- **2 to 3 ounces unsalted butter**
- **¾ cup soft brown sugar**
- **10 ounces Short-Crust Pastry (see Index)**

Preheat oven to 350°F. Peel, core, and slice the apples. Pare a 1½-inch strip of rind from the lemon. Put apples, lemon rind, butter and brown sugar in a heavy casserole. Cover the casserole and bake the apples in the oven for about 20 minutes, until tender. Remove from the oven and set aside to cool.

Increase oven temperature to 400°F. Cut off one third of the pastry and set aside, covered. Use remaining pastry to line a 10-inch pie plate. Roll reserved pastry to a rectangle 10½ × 8 inches. Cut the rectangle lengthwise into 10 strips to use for the lattice.

Drain the cooled filling and remove lemon rind. Spread apples evenly over the pastry. Moisten the edge of the pastry with cold water. Place 5 strips of lattice across the filled pie, then arrange 5 strips at right angles across the first strips. Seal the strips to the moistened edge. Bake the pie in the center of the oven for 20 minutes. Serve hot or cold, sprinkled with confectioners' if desired.

Variations: Use different spices (cinnamon, cloves, mixed spices) to enhance the flavor of the pie. For mincemeat and apple, spread a layer of mincemeat on the bottom of the pastry before filling with the apples. For rhubarb pie, substitute rhubarb for apples and an orange for the lemon; drain rhubarb well before spooning it in the pastry. Gooseberries, cherries and plums can be used as fillings; poach them in sugar syrup for half of the usual cooking time and drain well before spreading the fruit in the pastry.

Plum Pie

4 to 6 portions

- **2 pounds plums**
- **1 orange**
- **8 ounces Short-Crust Pastry (see Index)**
- **5 ounces soft brown sugar**
- **1 teaspoon ground cinnamon**
- **milk**
- **granulated sugar**

Preheat oven to 400°F. Adjust rack to the center position. Wipe the plums clean, remove stems, cut plums into halves, and remove the pits. Put plums in a bowl. Grate orange rind into the plums.

Roll out the pastry ¼ inch thick and 1½ inches larger than the top of a 4-cup pie dish. Cut a strip of pastry the same width as the rim of the dish from the edge of the rolled-out pastry. Moisten the rim of the dish and press the pastry strip on it.

Put half of the plums in the dish. Sprinkle on the sugar and cinnamon, then add remaining plums, piling them high in the center. Moisten the pastry rim and place the lid in position; press lightly to seal. Flute or crimp the edges at ⅓-inch intervals. Insert a knife under the edge of the pastry on opposite sides; raise the pastry slightly to make steam vents. Brush the surface of the pastry with milk and sprinkle it with granulated sugar to give the pastry a sweet glaze when baked.

Bake the pie for 20 minutes to set the pastry. Then reduce the oven temperature to 350°F and bake for 20 minutes longer.

Variations: For rhubarb pie, substitute 1-inch pieces of rhubarb for the plums. For gooseberry pie, use gooseberries; prick each one to prevent bursting during baking. Omit orange rind and cinnamon and use granulated sugar instead of brown sugar.

Nectarine Pie

6 portions

- **8 ounces Pate Sucrée (see Index)**
- **5 large nectarines**
- **1 lemon**
- **½ teaspoon freshly grated nutmeg**
- **¼ cup firmly packed brown sugar**
- **1 tablespoon unsalted butter**
- **1 tablespoon brandy**
- **1 egg yolk**
- **2 tablespoons milk**
- **2 tablespoons granulated sugar**

Prepare the pastry and chill it for 1 hour.

Preheat oven to 375°F. Cut off two thirds of the pastry and roll it out on a lightly floured board, or between 2 sheets of plastic wrap, to ¼-inch thickness and to a round about 11 inches across. Drop the round into a 9-inch pie dish and gently ease it into the base. Cut off excess dough. Set aside in a cool place.

Peel, pit, and slice the nectarines. Grate the lemon rind and squeeze the juice. Combine the nectarines, lemon rind, 1 tablespoon juice, the nutmeg and brown sugar in a bowl. Stir gently to mix. Spoon filling into the pastry-lined dish. Melt the butter and pour butter and brandy over the filling.

Roll out remaining pastry to a round large enough to cover the pie. Place over the filling and press the edges to seal. Flute or crimp the edges, and cut steam vents in the top. Mix the egg yolk with the milk and brush the top crust with the mixture. Sprinkle granulated sugar over the top.

Bake the pie for 30 to 40 minutes, until the pastry is crisp and golden brown. Serve immediately, or let the pie cool before serving.

GREY POUPON

Part Five

ENTERTAINING AT BRUNCH

Having friends for Sunday Brunch has become as American as apple pie and hamburgers. If you plan your menu wisely and cook ahead, there's no reason to rise with the Sunday dawn to make your preparations.

The table can be laid the day ahead, or if you plan on serving a casual menu that guests will eat seated in the living room, using lap trays, then make sure your napkins, cutlery, plates and glasses are at the ready, on a tray or serving table, or on the buffet table itself. A wise rule to follow if casual lap dining is indicated: Plan your meal so that guests can eat it easily with fingers and fork.

This simple yet elegant menu calls for tiny frittatas or vegetable-egg timbales baked in muffin tins or individual ramekins. Any seasonal vegetables, meats or fish make good fillings. These include a mildly seasoned spinach and onion mixture and a spicy sausage mixture. The frittatas are so small they can be popped onto the mouth with fingers. The roast quails (or game hens as an alternative) on buttery toast croutons can be roasted the day ahead, refrigerated, and warmed to room temperature several hours before the guests arrive. If you prefer them piping hot, cook them—they take less than 30 minutes—just before the guests arrive. The tomatoes, green preferred, red if that's all you can find, can be prepared at the last minute and kept warm in the oven. The salad ingredients can be washed, dried, and stored in plastic bags in the refrigerator. The dressing takes only a second to mix, so it does not need to be prepared in advance. As for the Bourbon Pecan Pie, it seems to taste better after a few days. The whipped cream—and pecan pie *does* cry out for lashings of whipped cream—should be prepared no more than 1 hour before the guests arrive.

The buffet table should have a centerpiece; whether this is a bouquet of artfully arranged seasonal flowers, vegetables or fruits, or a display of greenery such as rhododendron, laurel or podocarpus leaves in a lovely low bowl, is at the discretion of the hosts. A family with a spectacular collection of seashells might opt for a centerpiece of shells and dried flowers; if there is a baker in the family, a bountiful display of breads and rolls spilling out of a basket would be eye-catching and delicious as well.

Drinks? Coffee and tea, certainly, and wine and beer if this is your choice. Traditional brunch drinks include Bloody Marys (Virgin Marys are without alcohol), Screwdrivers (vodka and orange juice) and Mimosas (orange juice and Champagne). A nonalcoholic fruit punch should be on the menu as well. If the weather is warm you might want to include an iced herb tea.

Flowers make pretty garnishes for drinks: Roses are edible, so are nasturtiums, day lilies, borage flowers, violets, marigolds, chrysanthemums. Do not use flowers indiscriminately, for a very few are toxic and others are unpalatable. But a brilliant orange nasturtium swimming on an orange juice cocktail is memorable, its peppery taste delicious.

Since guests tend to linger at Sunday brunch, if you have plans for the evening be sure to mention this when you invite your guests; or else specify, "Come for brunch, 12:30 to 4:30."

Festive Sunday Brunch for Twelve

Spinach and Onion Frittata
Spicy Sausage Frittata
Roast Quails on Toast
Sautéed Green Tomatoes
Tossed Salad of Seasonal Greens
Bourbon Pecan Pie
Drink Suggestions:
Screwdriver, Bloody Mary,
Mimosa, Apple Cider Punch
Coffee, Tea

Brunch Drinks

The Bloody Mary and the Screwdriver have become the traditional brunch drinks across America, but you may want to investigate some regional and trendy specialties such as the Bullshot, the Strawberry Daiquiri, the Sazerac (a specialty of New Orleans, this), the Mint Julep (whose home is Kentucky), the Planter's Punch, Sangría and its wintertime partner, Mulled Red Wine. Here are recipes for three of the most popular—Bloody Mary, Screwdriver and Mimosa. With good, domestic Champagne selling at reasonable prices, this makes a very stylish way to usher in your guests.

Bloody Mary

1 drink

1½ ounces vodka
3 ounces tomato juice
juice of ½ lemon
2 dashes of Worcestershire sauce
pinch each of salt and pepper
dash of Tabasco® to taste

Mix all the ingredients, stir with ice, and serve.

Screwdriver

1 drink

1½ ounces vodka
4 ounces fresh orange juice

Mix ingredients, stir with ice, and serve.

Mimosa

1 drink

equal parts of fresh orange juice and Champagne

Pour orange juice into a Champagne glass and top with chilled Champagne.

Apple Cider Punch

1 drink

4 ounces fresh apple cider
2 ounces carbonated water
ground cinnamon

Combine cider and carbonated water. Sprinkle with cinnamon and serve chilled.

MARKET LIST

Meat and Fish

Hot sausage (1 pound)
Quails (12) or
Cornish game hens (6)

Fruits and Vegetables

Large onion
Spinach (½ pound)
Watercress (2 bunches)
Green tomatoes (12 small or 4 large)
Mixed salad greens (3 quarts)
Garlic (1 head)

Staples

Butter
Eggs
Heavy cream
Swiss cheese
Parmesan cheese
Paprika
Orégano
Salt
Pepper
Bread
Cornmeal
Wine vinegar
Olive oil
Sugar
Flour
Brown sugar
Dark corn syrup
Bourbon
Pecans

Spinach and Onion Frittata

14 frittatas

- 1 large onion
- 1 cup chopped cooked spinach
- 2 tablespoons butter
- 10 eggs
- ½ cup grated Swiss cheese
- ¼ cup grated Parmesan cheese
- ¼ cup heavy cream
- 1 teaspoon paprika
- 1 teaspoon salt

Peel and chop the onion. Drain spinach well. Sauté onion in butter until translucent. About 5 minutes before onion is done, add spinach and steam/sauté until hot and tender. Break the eggs into a large bowl and beat well. Add remaining ingredients and mix well. Pour the batter into well-buttered muffin pans or individual ramekins to make them two-thirds full. Bake in a preheated 325°F oven for about 20 minutes, until mixture is set. Unmold and serve at room temperature.

Spicy Sausage Frittata

14 frittatas

- **1 pound hot sausage, preferably Italian**
- **10 eggs**
- **¾ cup heavy cream**
- **1 teaspoon crumbled dried orégano**
- **½ teaspoon salt**

Cook the sausage and cut into thin slices. Beat the eggs and cream together in a large bowl. Add sausage, orégano and salt and mix well. Pour the batter into well-buttered muffin pans or individual ramekins to make them two-thirds full. Bake in a preheated 325°F oven for about 20 minutes, until mixture is set. Unmold and serve at room temperature.

Roast Quails on Toast

12 portions

- **12 quails, or 6 Cornish game hens**
- **12 slices of bacon**
- **5 ounces butter**
- **12 slices of white bread, 1 inch thick**
- **2 bunches of watercress**

Dress quails or Cornish hens; set giblets aside for another use. Wrap each quail in a slice of bacon, or each Cornish hen in 2 slices of bacon. Use 1 ounce of the butter to butter a pan large enough to hold birds in a single layer. Place birds in the pan and roast in a preheated 450°F oven for 10 minutes. Reduce oven temperature to 350°F and roast for 10 to 15 minutes longer for quail, for 20 to 25 minutes longer for Cornish game hens, or until birds are done to your taste.

If you have roasted Cornish game hens, use a sharp knife to split them into halves.

Make the toast croutons: Cut the crusts from thick slices of bread and toast them on both sides. Melt remaining 4 ounces of butter and sauté the toasts quickly, until golden. Serve the birds on the toast croutons, 1 quail or ½ Cornish game hen on each one. Garnish with watercress.

Sautéed Green Tomatoes

12 portions

12 small green tomatoes
1 cup milk
1 cup cornmeal
salt and pepper
bacon grease, butter or oil

Cut each tomato into 4 thick slices. Dip each slice into milk, then into cornmeal. Sprinkle lightly with salt and pepper. Sauté tomatoes in hot fat on both sides until golden. Keep them warm in a low oven.

Tossed Salad of Seasonal Greens

12 portions

3 quarts loosely packed mixed salad greens (romaine, Bibb, iceberg, chicory, escarole, watercress)
1 garlic clove
¼ cup wine vinegar
1 tablespoon prepared Dijon-style mustard
1 teaspoon sugar
¾ cup olive oil

Wash greens, dry, and tear into bite-size pieces. Peel the garlic clove and mash it with the side of a knife. Rub the garlic over the surface of a large salad bowl. Discard garlic. Combine vinegar, mustard, sugar and oil, and toss well with the salad greens just before serving.

Bourbon Pecan Pie

2 pies, 16 portions

Butter Pastry

- 2½ cups all-purpose flour
- 8 ounces butter
- 4 to 6 tablespoons ice water

Measure the flour into a bowl. Cut the butter into the flour with a pastry blender or 2 knives, until the particles are the size of oat flakes. Add just enough water to bind the pastry. Pat into a ball and let it rest in a cold place for 1 hour. Roll out the pastry on a floured board to 2 rounds and place each round in a 10-inch pie dish.

Bourbon Pecan Filling

- 8 ounces butter
- 1⅓ cups firmly packed brown sugar
- 1 cup dark corn syrup
- 5 eggs, beaten
- ½ cup Bourbon whiskey
- 3 cups shelled pecan halves
- 2 cups heavy cream, whipped

Combine all the ingredients except pecans and cream and mix well. Place 1½ cups pecan halves in the bottom of each pastry-lined pie dish. Pour in the filling. Bake in a preheated 450°F oven for 10 minutes. Reduce heat to 350°F and bake for 35 minutes longer, or until a knife inserted in the center comes out clean. Serve pies with whipped cream.

GORDON'S
VODKA
ONE LITER
GORDON'S
VODKA
perrier

INDEX